Examining Moses

From the Nile to the Promised Land

Jason Lee Willis

Lura Publications

Mapleton, MN

Lura Publications
803 Silver Street E.
Mapleton, MN 56065
www.lurapublications.wixsite.com/books
williswrites.com

Book Layout © 2017 BookDesignTemplates.com

Examining Moses/ Jason Lee Willis. – 2nd ed.
ISBN: 979-8-9903790-8-4

I'd like to dedicate this Bible study to my pastors, interns, and Sunday school teachers at First Lutheran Church in Colton, SD.

It seemed like the lesson was always about…Moses

Contents

STILL A NERD WITH A BIBLE

Again, I'm just a nerd with a Bible.

This is not going to be a research paper, a conclusive argument, an archeological manifesto, or anything even close to fancy. With the Internet at my fingertips and an aging set of Oxford textbooks on Egyptian history, I've just put together a study on Moses that made sense to me. There are tons of experts with authoritative claims about Moses, Egypt, and the whole Exodus time period, so the little thought bubbles found in this text are easily popped with the right pin, but my goal is to simply understand things better.

I'm a Christian, but since that is pretty generic, I'd characterize myself as a Luth-olic-a-tist, a baptized Lutheran, wannabe Catholic, a dabbler Baptist, and the "a" can stand for whatever loose hair I have on a certain day. Folks in my Bible studies know I love things to be as EPIC as possible, so if there is an outlandish view that requires far more faith than reason, that's usually where I gravitate. Like Peter and Andrew, I have more "fisherman" training than "Pharisee" training, but after two decades of teaching youth and adult Bible studies, I've found myself with many questions about the story of Moses and the Exodus.

Oh, I chose the old King James Version for the same reason I still teach Shakespeare in my English classes—to make you suffer (ah, a bit true). JK...I like to see the older English words to compare to modern language, which will often lead me to what the old Hebrew word might have been. Hope you enjoy the studies!

JLW

CHAPTER ONE

MIND THE GAP

Moses was a Prehistoric Caveman

(And...close the book)

Okay, I'm not desperately trying to get attention or twist the Bible into something strange. I'll pretend I didn't call Moses a caveman (until Chapter 6) because the word "caveman" immediately turned your Charlton Heston view of Moses into either a Neanderthal or Captain Caveman.

Neither was my intention.

Moses was born in 1446 BC!

(Ah, there is a fact that doesn't alarm)

How did we get that date?

It said it in a footnote of my Bible, delivered by a pillar of fire to the editorial staff. So how accurate was the 1446 BC date? That's what this chapter is going to focus on. I'm not here to mock a scholarly estimate, but only to argue that +/- 200 years is reasonable given the Biblical and historical accounts of the time.

So let's focus on the other word in my opening statement: prehistoric. When I began my quest to deeply understand the life and times of Moses, I drew upon my Hollywood, Hannah-Barbera, Vacation Bible Study coloring book interpretation of Moses and my many readings of Genesis and Exodus.

But when I decided to find other sources to enrich my understanding of the time period, I ran into a major problem. Moses was born in a prehistoric era.

Now, I'm not talking dinosaurs and wooly mammoths when I say prehistoric. When I wanted to enrich my understanding of the era of Jesus, it was easy because we had the accounts of the Romans, Egyptians, Parthians, and even the barbaric records from the wild British Isles because…"history" existed. A century of wiggle room can't happen during this time period because there is such a wealth of data. I couldn't argue George Washington was born in the 1300s because of the abundance of historical data.

When Moses was born, historical documentation was in its infancy, so I realized my quest to understand the time period was going to be much more challenging than understanding events during a more contemporary time. Yes, I trust what the Bible tells me, but even Christian scholarship about Moses can widely vary from denomination to denomination and from era to era. This frustrated me.

Yet any attempts to compare the "general" consensus about Moses to other "historic" timelines is problematic because "history" hadn't been invented yet. Let me explain.

Historical Graffiti

While Moses was "doing his thing," there were other cultures in the area that should have been recording the plagues described. Egypt. Canaan. Babylon. Greece. These cultures existed and did record things, but not the way we normally record history. During this time, nobody sat down to write a book on historical events. Instead, they treated history like wallpaper, chiseling and carving events onto stone. Historical graffiti?

Written historical documents became all the rage by 400 BC with writers like Herodotus (400ish BC), Berossus (300ish BC), Manetho (300ish BC) and Josephus (70 AD). Even if you trusted these accounts as Gospel, they missed Moses by a thousand years.

Which leaves us with Egypt (the villain in our story).

The "prehistoric" era used to be anything prior to written historical accounts. Homer's *Iliad* or Egyptian hieroglyphs existed with tales of eras long ago but how much fantasy and how much history did they contain? Was Polyphemus the Cyclops real? Ulysses? The Trojan War? While history now supports the Trojan War, accounts of one-eyed monsters or six-headed monsters are dismissed as prehistoric tales. Scoffers would lump *Exodus* into that category as well, yet would trust every detail written upon an Egyptian tomb. Homer and Moses made stuff up but Pharaoh Joe recorded accurate historic records!

See the irony?

When the Rosetta Stone was discovered in 1799 and decoded a few years later, everything about this "prehistoric" era was turned on its head. No one can claim the accounts found in hieroglyphics are modern fabrications, but this question needs to be answered: history according to whom?

Because Egyptian history is written on some old stone, scoffers would claim it is more reliable than the fluid 3,000 years of translations of Exodus. I see the point, but being old doesn't mean it was an accurately recorded fact. If Hitler had won WWII, human history would have been the history according to Hitler, right?

The Kings List, one of the ancient Egyptian records, stops at Ramses the Great, meaning what? It was the history of Egypt according to Ramses. The Table of Abydos is another ancient Egyptian record, built in the Temple of Seti. Who was Seti? Seti was the father of Ramses the Great, so...more history according to Ramses. The Table of Saqqara is another popular record, but guess what?

History according to Ramses.

So is there any obvious mention of Moses or the Hebrews in Egyptian history? History according to Ramses...uh, nope! Nada. Didn't happen.

It would seem I could not count on any other culture, especially Egyptian, to give me any insight into the times of Moses. So how did we get to 1446 BC?

Adding it All Up

Who needs other historical accounts? The Bible clearly says in the **Book of Dates** that the world was created 72 periods of time prior to the period of time when there was no time, added onto the time period in which it was written, with the assumption you'd include all of the periods of time since $(X+Y-Z/T)$.

Book of Dates Chapter 365, Verse 7: "The world is XXXX years old."

(sarcasm alert: there is no **Book of Dates).**

Anno Mundi is a Latin term that means World Years, and I am not the first to want to know how old the world is. At one time, I had a very confident guess that Adam was made in 3,972 B.C.

How? It seemed quite easy.

The Bible gives the "born, fathered, and died" dates for everybody from Adam to Joseph. Genesis 5 will get you from Adam to Noah, and Genesis 11 covers Noah to Abraham. The other patriarchs also have good dates, which gets you to a timeline of 2309 years. Exodus 12:40 adds 430 years onto this Anno Mundi calculation. Acts 13:20 says the Judges Era was about 450 years, which takes us to the "King" era. With Nebuchadnezzar appearing in non-Biblical history around 600 B.C., it all begins to add up neatly. While there is a "gap" in this dating system when we jump from the A.M. dates to the B.C. dates, you can throw a dart at any Pharaoh in the 18th dynasty (I picked Ramses and an Oxford history book), get a good B.C. date from it, add it to the Anno Mundi date from Genesis, and poof...3,972ish years B.C.

At the time, I hadn't yet pondered things like:

- o If God created a fully-grown Adam, why didn't he create a fully-grown world?
- o Adam "lived" for 930 years, but he didn't begin to die until he ate the fruit.
- o Is the "930" from his sin date?

- o If he was perfect, how long did he exist before he began to die?
- o How long did Adam exist before he grew lonely? Asked for a helper?
- o Day1=Light.
- o Day 4=Sun/Moon/Stars.
- o Day=huh?
- o Is Day 4 the creation of time? If so, then...huh?

Since the days of Jesus, scoffers have thrown LOTS of doubt onto these simple certainties, but back in the day, there were a few curious alternate timelines. The Romans, for example, had an Anno Mundi view that they were living in 5199 A.M. about the time of Jesus. Alexandrian scholars pegged the world at 5,500 B.C. However you interpreted or added the Hebrew Old Testament, 4,000 B.C. was certainly in the same ballpark.

Unfortunately, even the Hebrew texts were not as "absolute" as I once thought. In modern Bibles, you can find those darned asterisks and footnotes that will say things like "according to the Masoretic text" or "according to the Septuagint text."

Masoretic is the classic Hebrew translation, which is what I found in my NRSV version of Genesis. The Septuagint is also an old translation found during the time of Christ. Septuagint is the reference to 70 (sept) scholars who translated the texts into modern writing. Most of it is exactly the same, except for the dates in Genesis. These scholars debated and agreed that the dates in Genesis found in the Masoretic texts were "off" by a few zeros and it should read 5,500 BC. Why the change? Besides the old Masoretic text, the **Book of Enoch** (another dubious yet old text) claimed it would be 5,500 years from Adam to the Christ.

The Eastern Orthodox Church agreed and claimed Adam at 5,000 BC. Suddenly Christianity has a +/- of 1,500 years in the Anno Mundi.

Ah! Confusion! Why did I start digging, huh?

Now, I'm sticking to my 4,000 BC for Adam's sin (Adam was an adult man dropped onto an adult rock), but I brought up all the previous details to open the door to the fact that Moses can have a +/- 200 years of wiggleroom without it being heresy.

Let's try to get back to Moses

Dating during the 18th Dynasty

As you can see, looking to "external" sources for pinpointing *Exodus* can be wildly debated, so let's look at what details we get about dates within the Bible about the Moses story. Here is a quick summary of some of the cornerstone details (I'll discuss them all later in this book).

    A. Exodus 1:8—There was a regime change in Egypt after Joseph

    B. Acts 7:17—Yep, a regime change

    C. Acts 7:21—Moses was found by a royal female

    D. Act 7:22—Moses was trained, possibly as a warrior

    E. Acts 7:23—Moses fled/left when he was 40

    F. Exodus 4:19—Moses waited out an entire regime

    G. Acts 7:30—Moses returned to Egypt at the age of 80

    H. Deuteronomy 34:7--Moses died at the age of 120

Ah, that makes this undertaking seem a lot less daunting. With a +/- of 200 years, and these details to look for, all I need to do is slide around these 120 years of facts and contrast them

with the pharaohs recorded in Ramses' historical records (ew) to
see if anything jumps off the page.

The 1446 theory.

In many modern translations, the scholars will claim a date of
1446 B.C. based on the historical research established by comparing Egyptian (ew) and Babylonian records (also, ew). This is
the closest thing we have to a fact because, you know, prehistoric
records. It does bring up a pretty cool moment during the 18th
dynasty, Hatshepsut. According to this theory, Hatshepsut was a
rare instance of a female ruler, who was a little radical, and
might have even attempted a social coup by setting up her son.
Because of this, and the dates, it is very popular to see Hatshepsut as Detail C (from the list above), and the daughter of
Pharaoh. Heck, even Josephus seems to think this is the right
time period, and he's almost as good as Gospel (sarcasm alert). It
would make Thutmose III as the guy who chased Moses out of
Egypt, and Amenhotep II as the guy who wouldn't let the people
go. Peel away this regime, and there are some pretty cool details
that would work, and thus...1446 B.C. is pretty easy to sell.

However, if you read the "newly discovered" accounts of this
time period, it begins to feel like square pegs are trying to fit into
round holes. Where is the motivation? What makes any of them
stand out?

The 1991 theory

I also came across another scholar with a footnote who reasonably argued that the Pharaoh from Exodus was Amenemhet I, putting the Egyptian-Babylonian date at 1991 B.C. This theory squishes all of the Anno Mundi dates back quite a ways, but it also allows a lot of time for the Hebrews to grow from a small flock to a mighty nation. It also would turn Moses/Hebrews into a distant tale, which is why the Ramses' historians make nary a mention of them. See, no conspiracy theory with this one—just a distant memory. Of course, then you'd have to stretch the "wandering era" along with the "judges era," but hey, it doesn't conflict with the Egyptian-Babylonians, so...we're cool.

Two theories...+/- 500 years.

The Ramses Legend

Normally, I steer away from what is popular. Who has been a popular choice as the Exodus pharaoh for a long time? Ramses! Why? He's talked about in history, and there is this little reference to him in the text of Exodus 1:11 **"And they built for Pharaoh treasure cities, Pithom and Raamses."**

Ready for the clear water of the Niles to get muddied?

Well, if you look at 20 English translations, the spellings of **Raamses** will vary with uncertainty. Some scholars debate the meaning and spelling of the word. The reason? It is a female variation of a name. It is a name given in tribute. Some think it is a reference to a city built in the 19th dynasty, but that would push it WAY closer to B.C (eliminating Amenemhet I and Hatshepsut by a few hundred years=1300ish). It is also built in the delta (Goshen) instead of in the center of Egypt near Thebes (18th dynasty). Plus, there were no famous Ramses (do I plural it to Ramseses? How would you say that word?) until the 19th dynasty, so...

Problem!

The reason why I began with the "Mind the Gap" chapter is that however you slice it, there will be major problems trying to reconcile the dates. If you go with the Ramses theory, you have to squish the book of Joshua and Judges into less than the 450 years it seems to support. Plus, there is no good archeology. Plus, there are no clear hieroglyphics.

Can I ignore this conflict with the years?

Kinda.

Let me show you how nebulous dates can be. In *Exodus* 12:40, it seems to indicate that the Hebrews had been in Egypt for 430 years

[Exodus 12:40] Now the sojourning of the children of Israel, who dwelt in Egypt, was four hundred and thirty years. 41. And it came to pass at the end of the four hundred and thirty years, even the selfsame day it came to pass, that all the hosts of the LORD went out from the land of Egypt.

It later seems to support this fact in the book of Galatians:

[Galations 12:16] Now to Abraham and his seed were the promises made. He saith not, And to seeds, as of many; but as of one, And to thy seed, which is Christ. [17] And this I say, that the covenant, that was confirmed before of God in Christ, the law, which was four hundred and thirty years after, cannot disannul, that it should make the promise of none effect. [18] For if the inheritance be of the law, it is no more of promise: but God gave it to Abraham by promise.

So was that clock started with Abram leaving Ur or Jacob entering Egypt? Wow, so unclear!

Even within the Book of Exodus, which Moses authored, it strangely contrasts the obvious 430 years with Exodus 6:5, which lists off the lineage of Moses, which results in:

- o Levi=137 years of life
- o Kohath=133 years of life
- o Amram=137 years of life

If you add up those years, you only get 407 years, PLUS, we know that Levi (the son of Jacob) was not born in Egypt. Jacob and Levi came when the old patriarch was already very old. I'm not trying to find errors in the Bible, but I only want to argue that with all of these "prehistoric" dates, you need to have an open mind to allow a little bit of wiggle room.

Scoffers reject it because they want absolute black and white, verifiable, cross-referenced, and carbon dated kind of facts—it ain't happening.

I'm going to "examine" the Moses story by contrasting it with Ramses II, a.k.a. Ramses the Great, a.k.a. Ozymandias, a.k.a. Pharaoh (from Exodus). My reason for it, given what I've been given, is that it REALLY fits in the most epic and cool way I could want it to fit. Yes, I might be seeing the facts with rose-colored glasses (or glasses half full), but I hope you can at least open your mind to this cool narrative. Here is a preview of what happens when you line the Bible up with Ramses:

- o The 18th Dynasty Court fits the narrative
- o Ramses II fits the narrative
- o Baby Pharaoh fits the narrative
- o Exile Pharaoh fits the narrative

- Backdating fits with Joseph
- Backdating fits with Abraham
- Backdating fits with the Tower of Babel
- Backdating fits Adam's sin date.

If I'm wrong, well, then you'll learn some cool things about Egyptian history as well as some cool theories about Moses and the Hebrews. Buckle up.

CHAPTER TWO

THE SERPENT KINGS

Regardless of the exact date of the Exodus, there is a fascinating time period in Egyptian history that also occurs between the last page of Genesis and the first page of *Exodus*: the Hyksos Invasion.

Biblically, there is no mention of the Hyksos regime, but then again, there is little information given about a time period of 430 years. Let's look at what the Bible does give us. At the end of Genesis, Joseph belongs to the court of an anonymous pharaoh. The beginning of Exodus tries to bridge the two stories:

> **[Exodus 1:1] Now these are the names of the children of Israel, which came into Egypt; every man and his household came with Jacob. [2] Reuben, Simeon, Levi, and Judah, [3] Issachar, Zebulon, and Benjamin, [4] Dan, and Naphtali, Gad, and Asher. [5] And all the souls that came out of the loins of Jacob were seventy souls: for Joseph was in Egypt already. [6] And Joseph died, and all his brethren, and all that generation. [7]**

And the children of Israel were fruitful, and increased abundantly, and multiplied, and waxed exceeding mighty; and the land was filled with them.

So in year 1 of 430, we have around 70 Hebrews—give or take servants, etc.—migrating to Egypt during the seven bad years of famine. Verse 7 is terribly vague. How many years did they "wax exceedingly mighty" before things changed? By the time we get to year 429, we will have around 600,000 men (so a population of around 2 million) scattered along the Nile River (currently sustaining 100 million folks). There is little mystery in the previous section (other than why the English translator needed 3 verses to spit out 12 names, oofta!) That is quite a population boom that seems to be supported by Exodus 1.

Yet when did the boom take place?

And when did the Egyptians go from "knowing" Joseph to "not knowing" Joseph?

Exodus 1:8 brings up a major issue for me:

[Exodus 1:8] Now there arose up a new king over Egypt, which knew not Joseph.

If you follow Egyptian history, they get new kings (pharaohs) every decade or so. Sometimes, you can get multiple pharaohs in a single year. Regime change is not uncommon but the details surrounding this single verse can mean quite a bit. Was it the very next king? Did a hundred years pass? Two hundred? Three hundred? See, it just doesn't say.

During this vague 430 year period, (regardless of your choice for Pharaoh), something VERY DRAMATIC did happen in Egypt (and thus, to the Hebrews).

The Hyksos invaded.

The Hyksos Invasion

Unlike the "Hebrew Era" in Egypt, the hieroglyphic records actually deem the Hyksos rulers worthy of mention, which I find interesting. Today, the Hyksos people are a bit mysterious. Experts say they have "diverse" origins and "possibly" came from western Asia. Pretty vague. Just like the Egyptians, modern historians don't have a lot of details about who they were or where they came from. But we do know what they were like during their stay.

First, they invaded the delta (Goshen) and ruled at a city named, Avaris. This means that they invaded the heart of old Egypt and took out the previous dynasty. Northern/Lower Egypt is where all of the pyramids and wealth used to be found. It also means that the Hebrews were also enslaved along with the resident Egyptians.

Second, the Hyksos people were technologically advanced. On the old Anno Mundi timeline, the invasion happens around a 1,000 years after the Ark, giving humanity plenty of time to evolve and change. Remember how Genesis 10 describes the family trees, spreading out to be fruitful? Well, the Hyksos people finally came home, and when they did, they came with better techniques and weapons than the Egyptians. They were known for their horse culture, which is how they probably won their war against Egypt. Instead of a regular army, they were horse lords. In fact, they loved their horses so much that, upon death, they were buried with them. The horse and chariot revolutionized war in the region, but when they invaded in 1674 B.C. (Oxford dates), they were in a league of their own. Upon their horse and chariot, they also had powerful composite bows and battle-axes that helped them sweep down from...wherever.

Strangely, besides their military advantage, they were also known for their unique musical instruments (heavy metal was invented?). The Hyksos people arrived in Egypt worshipping storm gods, such as Hadad. Now this is curious because the Canaanite people (cue Imperial March theme) also worshipped Hadad. Was this just proximity and regional influence, or was there a connection between these two bad guy cultures. Later, the Hyksos were connected with far darker deities than storm gods, with their worship of an Egyptian god, Set(h). While it could be seen as appropriation, it should be noted that Seth was the god of death and chaos. This says a lot to me.

Along with their origins, historians and linguists have debated the meaning of the name Hyksos. Manetho, an early historian, believed their name translated as "King Shepherd." It is one of our oldest guesses (not sure if it makes it right). Josephus, who came onto the scene centuries later, also agreed with Manetho about it meaning "Shepherd Kings." Apion tells a much different tale, involving Osareph and a collection of 80,000 lepers. Some have speculated that Apion came across a veiled reference to the Hebrews and Exodus, but I am a little terrified to think of a leper horde...makes me think of a zombie army!

In recent years, historians have developed new theories about the name. Today, they believe the name should mean "rulers from foreign lands." Okay. Not as exciting as a zombie horde, but it makes sense. Some modern theorists view the migration as only coming from Palestine while others connect it to an Indo-Aryan expansion.

Indo-Aryan? Who are these guys?

Famine In All Lands

Before we explore the ramifications of this theory, let's go back to Genesis to remember the catalyst for all of this turmoil:

> **[Genesis 41:53] And the seven years of plenteousness, that was in the land of Egypt, were ended. [54] And the seven years of dearth began to come, according as Joseph had said: and the dearth was in all lands; but in all the land of Egypt there was bread. [55] And when all the land of Egypt was famished, the people cried to Pharaoh for bread: and Pharaoh said unto all the Egyptians, Go unto Joseph; what he saith to you, do. [56] And the famine was over all the face of the earth: And Joseph opened all the storehouses, and sold unto the Egyptians; and the famine waxed sore in the land of Egypt. [57] And all countries came into Egypt to Joseph for to buy corn; because that the famine was so sore in all lands.**

The scale of this situation is a bit stunning. Now remember: Egypt is the most fertile country on the planet. The Nile has tributaries that reach thousands of miles into the heart of Africa. If it rains in Africa, the Egyptians will get that water eventually. Yet Joseph is warned that Egypt will see seven years of famine.

Did the Nile dry up? Did the climate shift? Was there a volcanic explosion? For the Nile to NOT produce for seven years is a bit stunning. Not only was Egypt famished, but so too were other countries. This issue was global. See? It was a VERY BIG issue. Something happened to the earth that caused all humans and animals to suffer for seven years.

Luckily, Joseph packed away enough grain to not only feed Egypt but to also turn Egypt into the world's food bank, feeding Hebrews and others during this time. Lining up the Anno Mundi of Genesis and the Oxford B.C. dates, I have the Hebrews arriving in Egypt around 1734 B.C., which would give them 17 years before Jacob died, and another sixty years before the Hyksos invaded. If the famine was global, Indo-Aryan migration makes sense.

Heil Hyksos

The definition of Indo-Aryan is nebulous. Indo refers to India and Aryan...well, that definition depends if you are Germanic or not. Current historians and crazy historians differ. For the sake of being EPIC, let's allow a Germanic interpretation for just a minute. Remember how Hitler sent his genetic researchers to the Himalayas to try to rediscover the lost genetic code of the Aryan Race? Why did he do this? Well, he believed the Aryans were vastly superior. Even though his guys didn't find supreme beings, they did return with swastikas as a symbol for their Aryan quest.

Again, some modern historians interpret the Hyksos invasion as a bunch of bully shepherds coming from Palestine=dull. An Indo-Aryan migration is pretty EPIC, especially if you have a global catastrophe happening. Think of those post-apocalyptic, dystopian, zombie movies (or 2020)...when the going gets bad, mankind gets nasty. Sixty years after "the famine" affected the world, the Hyksos people had turned into a horse lord civilization capable of riding into your country and pillaging everything you had. Perhaps they did start out in India, but when crops began to grow again, these raiders did not turn the horse into a farm animal again, did they? They kept raiding.

If news of a paradise reached them, they now have a good reason to migrate. Considering all of the civilizations between India and Egypt, sixty years would be a reasonable amount of time.

There is also the Good-Evil symbolism to consider. The Hebrews/Israel are blessed by God not only with food and protection but also with the promise of the Christ. The Aryans are Hitler's ideal kinda folks. Regardless of where they come from, what do we see from the Hyksos people? Militaristic death worshippers. Beside the need to find a paradise, they might have been sent to crush the good guys.

Epic, huh?

These guys also would have been the ultimate deal-breaker. When the first Hyksos king arrived in Egypt, Joseph and the unnamed Pharaoh might have still been alive. I'd assume the Hyksos king would have killed the old ruler and (most) heirs, subjugated the previous administrators, and enslaved the people of Goshen, regardless of race. Whatever loyalty the old dynasty felt toward Joseph, God, and the Hebrews was shattered as the Hyksos army swept into southern/upper Egypt.

The Foreign Overlords

The old word for Hyksos, kekw chasut, also means *foreign overlords*, and that is certainly what life would have been like for the Hebrews. These guys didn't owe anybody anything. Now, it does baffle me that a nation of horse lords would decide to settle down, but that is what happened. On the Turin List, it records four kings ruling during the time from 1674 to 1567. The names of the kings were:

1. Sakir-Har (Sheshi)
2. Khyan (Aper-Anath)
3. Apophis (Samuqenu)
4. Khamudi (Sekhaerne)

These aren't just goofy names. These are sinister names.

Let me explain

Let's take King #3. Egyptian mythology changes from region to region and era to era. Although there is some semblance to the family tree found in Greek mythology, there are far more gods in the royal pantheon. One of the chief gods is Ra, the sun god. This is pretty obvious because sun in a desert country is a killer. So Ra was a pretty universal deity, but he had a counter-part—Apophis. Apophis was the serpent of destruction that battled each evening with Ra. When the sun went down, it was Apophis swallowing Ra to create a world filled of darkness. Yep, King #3 named himself after the symbol for darkness. It is like a conquering king renaming himself Satanny, Luciferman, Dev-ildude. There is a certain level of mocking and grandstanding in his choice. Willfully evil.

Another interesting name can be found in King #2. This one is a bit anachronistic. Ugaritic mythology is named after an ar-cheological dig at Ugarit where scholars found stories from Canaanite mythology. Anath is the violent, evil, murderous, wife-sister of Baal, the storm god found throughout the Old Testament. When King #2 named himself with an Anath reference, that means he either brought an older syste (Anath = Kali = Aryan) or he began a system that would grow into the Canaanite belief system. Or both?

Later, I'll talk more about Anath, but trust me when I say it is a foul name. Curiously, Ramses II will turn to Anath worship also and will even name a daughter after this foreign deity.

So the Hyksos regime ruled for a century under four different kings. After sweeping across the world, defeating the good guys, and taking up residence, the Hyksos regime lost their place in a rather silly turn of events.

The Hippo Decree

So King #4, Khamudi, really valued his sleep. He must have, for the sound of hippos belching each morning down by the river sent him into a rampage. As supreme commander, he decided that the hippo needed to die. He told his diplomat Seqenenre to begin wiping out the hippo population.

Little did he know...the hippo is a sacred animal to the Egyptians and involved in several old myths of creation. Plus, hippos are pretty cool and distinctly Egyptian. So when the diplomat rolls into southern Egypt with this announcement, they kill him rather than submit (THIS...IS...SPARTA, er...THEBES!)

The dynasties of the Joseph Era were in the north. The rebellion starts in the south, near Thebes, with an Egyptian by the name of Kamose. Because of his defiance, a three-year war begins, where the Egyptians take back southern Egypt. Did they get help from the nearby Nubians? Did they get help from Hebrews who had fled south to avoid the invaders? After three years, Egypt is again separated into a north/south or upper/lower or red/white division.

Ahmose I becomes the first Egyptian king/ruler/pharaoh in a century, and kicks off the 18th dynasty. Since all Egyptians dream of replicating the Scorpion King's actions of uniting the lands, Ahmose pushed the battle to the Hyksos. He invaded the north, displacing the Hyksos, and after another three years of fighting, wipes them out after trapping them in the Sinai wilderness.

Out of Africa

Even though the Hyksos nation vanished from history after losing this battle, it is doubtful that all the Hyksos people died. The women and children would have fled in advance, and based on where this story took them, I'd bet they went into Israel/Palestine. There are a few scholars that believe the story of the Exodus is just the story of the Hyksos expulsion. From the shepherd kings to the migration route, it did give me pause, but there are numerous alignment and theological issues that do not seem to fit with this theory.

In the Oxford-Ramses timeline, it will still be another 200 years before the Hebrews leave Egypt, allowing the Hyksos people time to repopulate and become another nation. Here is a quick Oxford-Ramses timeline:

- o 1734 BC=Jacob and Israelites arrive in Egypt
- o 1717 BC=Jacob dies (during Dynasty 14)
- o 1674 BC=The Hyksos invade Egypt and claim the Delta
- o 1663 BC=Joseph dies

- 1567 BC=The Theban princes (Kamose/Amose) drive out the Hyksos (with coalition of Nubian/Hebrews?)
- 1567 BC=Hyksos survivors settle in vacant Palestine
- 1304 BC=Hebrews leave Egypt

There is still quite a bit of time after the Hyksos leave, isn't there? 263 years can change a lot. Let's go back to **Exodus** and look at how those years were described.

[Exodus 1:8] Now there arose up a new king over Egypt, which knew not Joseph. [9] And he said unto his people, Behold, the people of the children of Israel are more and mightier than we: [10] Come on, let us deal wisely with them; lest they multiply, and it come to pass, that, when there falleth out any war, they join also unto our enemies, and fight against us, and so get them up out of the land.

First, the description of a new king would have fit anywhere on the 430 year timeline, but during that time, there were two massive regime changes. The first was when the 14th Dynasty northerners (Joseph's guy) lost Egypt to the Hyksos. The second was when the Hyksos rulers lost to the 18th dynasty southerners from Thebes.

Let's put on Theban colored glasses to look at this verse. The new king is Amose I, who did not know Joseph, right? He just united Egypt, defeated the Hyksos, but has a real problem—Hebrews outnumber Egyptians. Now, I believe the Hebrews most likely helped in the rebellion and have proven to be worthy allies. Yet, the threat remains.

The solution?

A **wise** plan. The plan must be shrew because if they bungle it, the Hebrews could easily rise up and overwhelm them by sheer numbers. Ahmose does not want to purge them from Egypt because of "enemies." Could this be the threat of the Hyksos remnant? A new Hittite nation? A threat from Nubia? Don't know. But the threat remains, which is why he chooses to keep the Hebrews around so they don't turn on him. His plan is to keep them and subjugate them, which is why it needed to be a "wise" plan.

It was also a patient plan.

If this is said right after the war with Hyksos, it would take generations before the Hebrews transitioned from military heroes to working slaves. During my Horemheb research, I read how tax burdens were used to legally create slaves. Remember, Jacob and his 70 came into Egypt as almost royal guests. After the Hyksos wars, the Hebrews were still a threat. By the time we get to Moses' birth, they are all slaves. So what happened?

My theory is that the "wise plan" hatched by Ahmose I was to begin taxing the Hebrews. Generation A received a small tax. Generation B received a higher tax. Generation C, quite used to taxes and life in Egypt, received a huge burden. They probably faced the choice of either paying their taxes or leaving the country. This is after hundreds of years of living in Egypt. None of them knew Israel, and if they did, heard rumors of who now lived there. Fight or pay taxes. I'd bet they found a way to pay taxes.

The Horemheb theory is that the tax burden was put on the children. Seems outrageous? Look at our current national debt. No way? Look at our social security program. It is easy to pass the buck to the next generation. So Generation D would have been born slaves to all the folks who could not afford to pay the bill.

It was a wise plan.

[Exodus 1:11] Therefore they did set over them taskmasters to afflict them with their burdens. And they built for Pharaoh treasure cities, Pithom and Raamses. [12] But the more they afflicted them, the more they multiplied and grew. And they were grieved because of the children of Israel. [13] And the Egyptians made the children of Israel to serve with rigor: [14] And they made their lives bitter with hard bondage, in mortar, and in brick, and in all manner of service in the field: all their service, wherein they made them serve, was with rigor.

So verse 1:11 covers two centuries of this policy afflicting them. There are a few other things in this passage I'd like to point out. The reference to Pithom and Raamses is strangely anachronistic. According to the Hatshepsut Timeline (1446 BC), Moses would have written this verse a century before the two cities existed. Raamses is not misspelled, but it is a name variation of the guy who commissioned the building, Ramses the Great, who did not take the throne until 1304 BC. Now, you could argue name meanings and make this bit of anachronism vanish, but the other fun detail is that the Hebrews made bricks. Most of ancient Egypt was made with carved stone, but during the 18th Dynasty, especially the Valley of the Kings era, bricks were very popular. I believe that this supports the Oxford-Ramses timeline more than the other way around.

CHAPTER THREE

THE EGYPTIAN COURT

In examining the story of Moses, I wanted to understand the motivations and influences of the world around him. I wanted a little context for the time period. Now, as I explained in chapter one, picking a date and pharaoh is pretty open to interpretation; however, once selecting a pharaoh at the Exodus, there is a pretty clear timeline described in the Bible to hold up against the Egyptian facts (yes, I know, I called them facts).

I've chosen Ramses the Great as "the guy," fully aware of the flaws in my candidate, but when I look at my Oxford textbook, I found some pretty cool alignments within the 18th Dynasty that really brought the story to life. This chapter will profile some of the characters found in the two sources.

Before we begin, I'd like to talk about some of the mythology and beliefs held by the Egyptians. Yes, pharaohs were seen as gods upon the earth. Their divine quality was usually seen as being passed down by Horus (the hawk guy, son of Osiris). Another popular connection to the gods was through the goddess Sekhmet (a lioness). This belief was a bit different since Sekhmet was a female deity, and because of this, the "divine qualities" were given through female bloodlines.

The Hebrews, by contrast, were fairly patriarchal. Inheritance was normally passed down from father to first-born son. Of course, the strange family trees given in Matthew and Luke were 90% patriarchal with a few exceptions thrown in. Jesus (of course) was not a first-born son of a first-born son of a first-born son. The legal and biological trail from Adam to Joseph brought in unique females like Tamar, Rahab, Ruth, and Bathsheba, along with a host of second sons. But...mostly patriarchal, right?

Egyptian Legalese

Egyptian beliefs were not nearly as crisp. Let's create a hypothetical family. Let's say Pharaoh Joe and Queen Katherine had a bunch of kids. The eldest, Prince Jackie, is born to inherit his father's property and stuff. The other sons (Prince Tito, Jermaine, Marlon, Randy, and Michael) might get a few nice things in the will, but are technically threats to Prince Jackie because if Jackie fell in a well and died, then Tito would be next up. Sounds just like the Hebrews, so far, right?

The Sekhmet belief made it a bit more complicated. Since Sekhmet was a female deity and Horus was a male deity, the DAUGHTERS of Pharaoh Joe were blessed with divine gifts also. So Princess LaToya and Janet might not get the throne, but they were very special in their own rights.

This is where things get creepy (aside from my extended metaphor).

If Pharaoh Joe wanted to prevent his family from tearing itself apart, he took a page from the Osiris and Isis playbook. Just like the Greek gods, Osiris and Isis were brother and sister and also husband and wife (and parents to Prince Horus). If Prince Jackie married Princess LaToya, then their child would have legal and divine authority. The non-Fantastic Five would be pushed away because of this creepy power-marriage and the dynasty would be strong (aside from the birth defects). This is what the first Pharaoh of the 18th Dynasty did. Ahmose the First married his sister, who had the supercool title Ahmose-Nefertari (a union of more than names, get it?).

However, if Pharaoh Joe had favorites, say his youngest son Michael, and wanted to place him in a position above the other heirs, he would allow a marriage of Michael and Janet (yep, threw up in my mouth a bit) as a way to set him above Prince Jackie and his non-sister wife. Trouble would be brewing by the time we get to the grandkids, right?

Well, that is the mess Moses was born into and the reason why the Hebrews needed 10 Commandments as well as the Book of Leviticus to reset their moral compasses.

A New Egypt

During the 18th Dynasty, Egypt was restored but a new capital was chosen by the new dynasty (who did not know the promises of Joseph/Hebrews). They built the city of Thebes, which is hundreds of miles south of Goshen, where Cairo and most pyramids are found. From the day the Hyksos lost (1567 BC) to the day Moses and the Hebrews left (1304 BC), the Egyptians had more than two centuries to build a new palace-city.

Thebes was isolated from a quick invasion from Hyksos, Minoan, Philistine, Canaanite, Hittite, Greek, or Roman army (yep, the north got conquered a lot) while also using the Nile River as an international highway to the nations to the south like Nubia and Aksum.

Today, we know all sorts of stuff about the 18th Dynasty because of their complex graveyard known as the Valley of the Kings. Unlike the tedious pyramids, which took a long time and a lot of skill to build (plus, we are out of aliens, giants, or angels to help build new ones), the 18th Dynasty utilized a barren valley a few miles from the Nile for the tombs, which were dug into the cliffs. The Valley of the Kings holds sixty "famous folks" from this time period, preserving their deeds upon the stones of the tomb.

Okay, here are the Moses details again:

- o   He was 120 years old when he died.
- o   40 years in the wilderness.
- o   Thus...80 years old when he began the Exodus.

If Ramses was the Pharaoh, then all you need to do is go backwards from Ramses to see how they match up with the life of Moses.

Moses was 40 when he killed an Egyptian and fled Egypt.

The Pharaoh? Horemheb.

Go back another 40 years, and Moses is an infant.

The Pharaoh? Amenhotep III

So this is the place where we're going to dig a little deeper.

Amenhotep III

Remember, this is the guy who will kill all the babies, so I needed to understand the motivations of a dude this obviously evil. Unfortunately, the Egyptians do not portray him as a Dark Lord. A thousand years after his death (almost to the Cleopatra era), he was still worshipped as a fertility god, which is a strange paradox for a man who murdered babies. His reign is described as being filled with peace and affluence, with bumper crops unseen in history. Amenhotep was a robust, warrior king during his reign who brought back the classic worship of Egyptian gods. His name, for example, is homage to the creator god Amun. He is credited with rebuilding "middle Egypt" around Thebes and for also rebuilding the royal family system.

Remember Pharaoh Joe's mess?

Well, Amenhotep III (A-3? Trey?) came up with a new policy that allowed royal daughters to marry "non-royal men." The reason? Apparently…selfishness. He worried that his own family might rise up and dethrone him. Instead of allowing a Michael-Janet power-marriage, he legalized it so that his daughters could marry commoners-with-clout (you know, generals, advisers, rich dudes). Thus, his sons were left weak and his sons-in-law would have his back. This policy also allowed him to create alliances with neighbors, and biologically, it probably helped with the weird incest issues of the last two centuries.

It appears as if Amenhotep III had two sons and at least one famous daughter. His eldest son and heir to the throne was named Thutmose. In some ancient scripts, he is described as "the real King's son," which has baffled historians a bit. Amenhotep III's younger son was later known as Amenhotep IV (which tells you something) and then called Akhenaten (I'll explain later). A-4 must not have been trusted because he was married to a northern gal instead of his sister. The sister was named Mudnodjme and she married a non-royal southerner named Horemheb (yep, he's a villain). There certainly might have been other kids, but these were the major political players.

By the time Amenhotep III was an older man, Thutmose was married and so was A-4. If the boys did not produce a male heir, the Theban line would come to an end, so Amenhotep III held the throne until the bitter end. Ultimately, Thutmose did not become Pharaoh when his pop died, so something had to have happened? Did he lose favor and was passed over? Unlikely. Did he commit treason and come down with a case of the Herods? Possibly. Was it an assassination? Could be, but not likely once I got to know his brother. Just an accident? Likely. But later, the traditional Theban Egyptians would have looked back on a regime that could have been. I think this is why he is called "the real King's son" as in "the right prince." Thutmose would have been groomed for a throne he never sat upon. Instead it went to A4.

So now that we've met Amenhotep III, let's hold a Biblical mirror up to this figure and compare Exodus and the anonymous pharaoh. In Exodus, we read:

[Exodus 1:8] Now there arose up a new king over Egypt, which knew not Joseph. [9] And he said unto his people, Behold, the people of the children of Israel are more and mightier than we: [10] Come on, let us deal wisely with them; lest they multiply, and it come to pass, that, when there falleth out any war, they join also unto our enemies, and fight against us, and so get them up out of the land. [11] Therefore they did set over them

**taskmasters to afflict them with their burdens. And they built
for Pharaoh treasure cities, Pithom and Raamses. [12] But the
more they afflicted them, the more they multiplied and grew.
And they were grieved because of the children of Israel. [13]
And the Egyptians made the children of Israel to serve with
rigor:**

How does it stack up?

A.   Amenhotep would not have known Joseph

B.   Amenhotep ruled over a prosperous era

C.   Dealing with a majority minority would have taken generations.

D.   The enemies were the defeated Hyksos

E.   Raamses is anachronistic unless Moses wrote this post-Ramses the Great

So if verses 8-13 fit the narrative nicely, let's look at the specific crimes of Amenhotep III from Exodus:

**[Exodus 1:15] And the king of Egypt spake to the Hebrew
midwives, of which the name of the one was Shiphrah, and the
name of the other Puah: [16] And he said, When ye do the office
of a midwife to the Hebrew women, and see them upon the
stools; if it be a son, then ye shall kill him: but if it be a
daughter, then she shall live. [17] But the midwives feared
God, and did not as the king of Egypt commanded them, but
saved the men children alive. [18] And the king of Egypt called
for the midwives, and said unto them, Why have ye done this
thing, and have saved the men children alive? [19] And the
midwives said unto Pharaoh, Because the Hebrew women are
not as the Egyptian women; for they are lively, and are
delivered ere the midwives come in unto them. [20] Therefore
God dealt well with the midwives: and the people multiplied,
and waxed very mighty. [21] And it came to pass, because the**

midwives feared God, that he made them houses. [22] And Pharaoh charged all his people, saying, Every son that is born ye shall cast into the river, and every daughter ye shall save alive.

Now, I don't have anything insightful or witty to say about the midwives except that they are pretty cool. It also seems to be part of a systematic, calculated attempt to keep the Hebrews under control (beginning with the start of the Theban Dynasty). Any attempts to thwart the lively nature of the Hebrew population failed. In the final verse, the anty is upped. "His People" means any and all Egyptians. Racism is promoted. Egyptian vs. Hebrew policies begin. It is no longer about taxes and staying in a fertile valley; it is now about survival.

So as not to upset the gods, the male babies are thrown into the river. Why? Killing a child could be seen as a sin in the eyes of Osiris, Aten, or GOD. The Greeks did this all the time. Oedipus had his ankles bound so he could die of exposure. Whose fault? The gods. Here, Amenhotep does not SLAUGHTER like Herod did in Bethlehem, he has the male babies chucked into the river so FATE could decide.

Sneaky policy.

Before we meet Moses in the next verse, let's meet a new Egyptian, one who has personal stakes in the production of male babies.

Princess Nefertiti

Perhaps the most famous face in Egyptian history, Nefertiti was almost wiped from history by religious zealots. It is a wonder I can even tell you her story in the present, but thanks to "believers" way back in the day, enough traces of this enigmatic figure have survived. Nefertiti was a princess-in-law who later became queen, through her marriage to Amenhotep IV. Their rule is the most vilified regime in all of Egyptian history, and shortly after it ended, zealots tried to wipe them from Egyptian history.

Gnarly, huh?

Before we talk about WHY they were hated, let's look at some basic details about who she was. As with most Egyptians, there are numerous titles written to fill any ego with the belief that he or she might be descended from the gods. Here are three of those monikers:

"The Beautiful Woman has Come"

"Lady of Two Lands"

"Mistress of Upper and Lower Egypt"

The first title is pretty obvious. When a German archeologist discovered her bust in a workshop in the ruined city of Amarna, few knew the details of Akhenaten and Nefertiti. But beginning in 1912, the world learned not only that she existed but that she was beautiful as well. Her stunning beauty (or the work of the sculptor) drove curiosity into a Queen that seemed to be erased from the Valley of the Kings. Sure enough, there had been a cover-up three thousand years ago. Amarna was an abandoned center of worship that had been torn down by traditionalist zealots. The original sculptor had probably kept the bust as a keepsake since all the others had already been systematically destroyed following the regime change. It's akin to a Republican keeping a Nixon '72 statue after Watergate. Both in text and in effigy, Nefertiti was really beautiful, but what does the whole phrase imply? Has Come? That implies there had been a wait. Who would be waiting?

Well, the next two monikers shed light on the first meaning. Lady of Two Lands and Mistress of Upper and Lower Egypt tell us quite a bit about her. Let's quickly simplify four hundred years of Egyptian royalty:

Dynasty 14: Northern Egyptians, aka Lower Egypt, aka Delta, Delta, Delta.

Dynasty 15-17: Hyksos, aka Foreigners, aka Evil, evil, evil.

Dynasty 18: Southern Egyptians, aka Upper Egypt, aka Thebes, Thebes, Thebes.

Lady of TWO Lands? LOWER Egypt?

Since the mythological era of the Old Kingdom, Egypt has been separated into two parts. A long time ago, a figure known as the Scorpion King (I swear I'm not making this up), fought against an evil tyrant to unite Egypt. Since that era, the goal of every pharaoh is to wear the crown of a united Egypt. The red crown and white crown worn together are the symbol of unity. Now do you see the significance of Nefertiti's moniker?

IF she was a member of the Theban royal family, how would she be from two lands? She would only be from D18. IF she was a foreign born princess, then how could she bring both lands under one banner? Yes, she could be from Cuba, and marrying D18 princeling A4, she would later become a queen of "Two Lands." However, her third moniker, "Mistress of Upper and Lower Egypt," seems to dismiss that idea as well.

To puzzled historians, Nefertiti is seen as a foreigner, Egyptian, and royal because she most likely belonged to the remnants of Dynasty 14. What happened to them? Hyksosed. Yep, the royal family either died in battle or was slaughtered during the invasion, but it is unlikely that all of them were Romanoffed. Think of Nefertiti as our Anastasia. The survivors of D14 would have lost their freedom and joined the Hebrews, Deltans, Thebans, and Nubians as slaves under Hyksos rule. When it ended, the Thebans had power and D14 had freedom. If the Delta was their home, they would have rebuilt their estates and gone on with their lives. Two centuries later, they might have become wealthy enough to be seen as a political threat to A3. His solution? Amenhotep III most likely wanted to use the marriage to strengthen his hold on ALL OF EGYPT.

The Mistress of Upper and Lower Egypt!

However, there were many strings attached to this marriage. If Nefertiti did come from D14, then she has other family members who also have old royal blood. If she has D14 blood, that means she was a descendent of the pharaoh who allied himself with Joseph and the Hebrews! This Delta House has control over the Hebrews now, and can keep D18 in power if given a bit more power. Having survived the Hyksos purge, D14 would have been a bit crafty and politically savvy. Sure enough, Nefertiti has a famous father, Ay, and a famous brother, Smenkhkare (We'll talk about them later). Delta House needed to be placated but not empowered. That is why A3 most likely allowed his SECOND son to marry Nefertiti while planning on giving the throne to Thutmose.

That is not what happened.

Foster Parents

Exodus introduces "Pharaoh's daughter," but I'd like to speculate that she is NOT a biological daughter but a legal daughter, a daughter-in-law. Could Thutmose have been married to his sister (princess!)? Sure. Could A3 have had an anonymous daughter married to a nobody? Sure. Yet later, in the Book of Hebrews, Moses seems to have a BIG choice presented to him. This choice is only significant if he rises to power along with his foster mom and dad. Again, if I put my pin in Ramses the Great (and go back 80 years), there might have been other biological daughters of A3, but none of them fit so dramatically as Nefertiti, so I'm sticking with the daughter-in-law interpretation.

If there is a princess, there must be a prince. While I'm not sure what he was called prior to becoming pharaoh, he was Prince B in ascension. When the babies were being thrown in the water, he was still Prince B and was married to Nefertiti. He did not expect to become Amenhotep IV, and certainly, he did not plan on becoming the infamous Akhenaten. He was only Prince B.

It is unsure how he would have taken his marriage to somebody outside D18, and it is unclear who Prince A, Thutmose, married. Once thing that was clear—Nefertiti bore a bit of a curse!

Praying for a Son

It would be nice to think of a Disney marriage, but for all intents and purposes, it was initially a political marriage. With A3 living a long, prosperous life, Prince A and Prince B were married and began to produce grandchildren. Think of it as a race to produce a male heir. While I don't know what was going on in the marriage bed of Thutmose (probably mutant incest babies), records indicate that Prince B and Nefertiti were plagued with daughters!

For a moment, rethink how Amenhotep would have looked at his grandchild situation. Everything he has built is lost if Prince A or Prince B do not have a male child. While Nefertiti is fertile she is not providing the right gender. Prince A? Thutmose vanishes from history about this time. Babies would have been a source of agitation for Amenhotep III, so that is ANOTHER reason why this psychopath promoted a genocide policy.

It was also a serious problem for Nefertiti. If she can't produce a male heir, Amenhotep III will look away, D14 folks will feel shame and miss an opportunity for power, and Prince B might have to find a new wife. Now, this is where I think they might have been Disney-married. According to historical records, Akhenaten and Nefertiti had numerous daughters:

> Merit-aten
> Meket-aten
> Ankhesenpa-aten
> Nefer-Neferu-aten Tasherit (that's a mouthful)
> Neferu-Neferu-Re (imagine calling them for supper)
> Setepen-Re

That's a bunch of girls. Now, I don't know exactly how many were born prior to mom and dad becoming Pharaoh and Queen, but based on whom they marry, I'd guess a bunch of them. With 9 months bun-oven time, their first few years of marriage would have been seen as a failure, especially for Nefertiti.

What would a girl do?

Pray!

Who would she pray to?

There were a lot of fertility gods in Egypt. Take your pick: Amun, Bastet, Heqet, Heryshaf, Isis, Nesent, or Min. See the problem? Were her religious beliefs similar to Dynasty 18 or Dynasty 14? Hmm? Something cool to ponder is that Hapi was the God of the Nile, and the annual flooding of the Nile brought rich silt to the river's banks. Hapi delivered fertility each year. Regardless, Nefertiti turned to prayer, only to have THIS happen:

[Exodus 2:1] And there went a man of the house of Levi, and took to wife a daughter of Levi. [2] And the woman conceived, and bare a son: and when she saw him that he was a goodly child, she hid him three months. [3] And when she could not longer hide him, she took for him an ark of bulrushes, and daubed it with slime and with pitch, and put the child therein; and she laid it in the flags by the river's brink. [4] And his sister stood afar off, to wit what would be done to him.

Clever girl! The royal decree was that all male Hebrew babies had to be cast in the river. Moses's biological mother obeyed the decree with a twist: she cast him in the river with an ark of bulrushes and Miriam nearby. Let the gods decide? Well, we have a bit of Fate AND Free Will going on in the above verses. Another thing to note is that like King David, Moses is marked from birth with unnatural beauty (check other translations).

Now look at it from the perspective from Princess Nefertiti:

[5] And the daughter of Pharaoh came down to wash herself at the river; and her maidens walked along by the river's side; and when she saw the ark among the flags, she sent her maid to fetch it. [6] And when she had opened it, she saw the child: and, behold, the babe wept. And she had compassion on him, and said, This is one of the Hebrews' children. [7] Then said his sister to Pharaoh's daughter, Shall I go and call to thee a nurse of the Hebrew women, that she may nurse the child for thee? [8] And Pharaoh's daughter said to her, Go. And the maid went and called the child's mother. [9] And Pharaoh's daughter said unto her, Take this child away, and nurse it for me, and I will give thee thy wages. And the woman took the child, and nursed it. [10] And the child grew, and she brought him unto Pharaoh's daughter, and he became her son. And she called his name Moses: and she said, Because I drew him out of the water.

Official policy is to kill boy babies, but Nefertiti has been praying (to the river) to bless her womb with a male. Now, she sees Hapi deliver a beautiful male child right to her bathing spot. A Theban princess might have had her maidens dump it into the water, but a Deltan woman would have had a four-hundred-year relationship with Hebrews since Joseph. Ah! Notice how the Princess KNOWS it is Hebrew but does not have an issue with it? Peculiar for anybody but a D14, Deltan, foreign princess such as Nefertiti.

It was a blessing from the gods!

While it is nice to think of a dimwitted Nefertiti being gullible enough to save Moses because Hapi the River God gave her Moses (even though it was clearly Miriam), I'd like you to consider another radical option: Nefertiti was a BELIEVER!

The Faith of Nefertiti

Our baby-in-a-basket ends up living to the ripe old age of 120 and also writes the Pentateuch (Torah/First Five Books of the Bible). In doing so, he includes a scene where he asks God his name, only to receive a coded answer. Literally, the answer was YHWH (without the vowels); however, Moses himself goes and uses a whole bunch of other names. Why would he do that? He asked God his name, and if he got a literal answer, shouldn't he just use that name each and every time? But that is not what we get from Moses. Instead, he used Elohim, El Shaddai, Addonai, and a bunch of variations of YHWH (we'll talk about this again later).

I bring this up because we are fond of using the word "GOD." Anything but GOD sounds like heathen idol worship to us, right? It wasn't until Moses was 80ish that anybody asked GOD for a name, so whatever they used before this was simply a fabrication or nickname, right? For crying out loud, what did the Hebrews use before the official YHWH?

If Nefertiti was a northern Delta girl, and also an obvious friend to Hebrews, then she might have an open mind because of her beliefs. In studying Egyptian mythology, it is hard to follow a single family-tree plot like the Greeks or Norse had because the Egyptian gods would morph from dynasty to dynasty. As a result of conquest and time, there are several popular creation stories. When I came upon the Heliopolis (Delta) mythology, I was startled by the similarity of the stories.

Atum is known as "the Complete One" and emerges from the primeval waters, Nun. His first act was to bring about "The Island of Creation."

TRANSLATION: "And the Spirit of God was hovering over the face of the waters" and "Then God said, 'Let the waters under the heavens be gathered into one place, and the dry land appeared.'" Nefertiti and Moses would have shared a creation story, but it gets even better...

Since Atum was alone in the world, he had to create other gods FROM HIS OWN SUBSTANCE, and he proceeded to give birth to his son Shu (God of the Air) by spitting him out and to his daughter Tefnut (Goddess of Moisture) by vomiting her forth. Okay, that was weird.

TRANSLATION: **"Let there be light"** and **"bore a male child who was to rule all the nations with a rod of iron."** Back in the days of Constantine, the early Christians got together at Nicaea to work on a creed. One of the sticking points was the definition of Jesus Christ as SON. One camp argued that Jesus is OF SIMILAR substance as God; another camp argued and won (Gospel of John) that Jesus was OF THE SAME substance as God. Elohim is a plural world. The triad of Atum, Shu, and Tefnut is very similar to Elohim (God, Holy Spirit, and Christ). Shu is the God of the Air while the Holy Ghost is...complicated (fire and air?) Tefnut is a physical manifestation described as a bloody lion holding a staff; Jesus is a physical manifestation, the Lion of Judah, and will/does holds a rod of iron. Nefertiti would readily accept the Christ concept.

The Heliopolis mythology gets even better. From the triad comes two created figures: Geb and Nut. Geb was the earth god while Nut was his consort, who was created when she was separated from him. The arrival of Geb and Nut officially completed all the cosmic elements necessary for creation.

TRANSLATION: **"And the Lord God formed man of the dust of the earth, and breathed into his nostrils the breath of life, and the man became a living being"** and later Eve was created from Adam's rib. Geb and Nut=Adam and Eve.

Want more? Well, Geb and Nut become parents of two sons, Osiris and Seth. Seth becomes jealous of his brother, so he murders Osiris and buries his body to hide it.

TRANSLATION: **"Now Cain talked with Abel his brother, and it came to pass, when they were in the field, that Cain rose up against Abel his brother and killed him"** and later buried his body in the ground.

There is another story that is a bit weird but also insightful. Osiris's sister-wife Isis seeks revenge through her son Horus, who fights against the evil Seth. A tribunal is held. Osiris is allowed to be resurrected in the underworld and Horus becomes king of the living and Seth is banished.

TRANSLATION: God said to Cain, **"A fugitive and a vagabond you shall be on the earth"** which leads Cain to the Land of Nod. Jewish folklore talks about Cain marrying his sister-wife Luluwa while Seth (3rd born, not Seth=evil god) marries his sister-wife Aklia. Abel would have been the first soul in Sheol, and during Easter, Christ would have harrowed Abel's soul and brought it back to Heaven.

Yup, Nefertiti could EASILY have been a BELIEVER.

An Influence on Dad

Some scholars and scoffers could also argue that Moses was influenced by HER, and that the origin of the Hebrew God is only a rip-off of the monotheistic Aten created during the rule of Akhenaten and Nefertiti. I see it the other way. I believe that Nefertiti might have had some misguided Atum beliefs, but after spending time with Moses' mother and sister, turned into a believer herself. Her belief might have gone horribly wrong with the promotion of Aten, but it is quite a coincidence that the only era of monotheism in the history of Egypt happened at exactly the same time as Moses.

Regardless, the Egyptian court is in a very strange place when Amenhotep III dies. After hundreds of years, the Deltans have a Queen with Nefertiti. Her influence is seen immediately with her Theban husband. He takes his father's name and becomes Amenhotep IV, crowning himself under Amun; however, the building projects during his first five years are NOT named after Amun but after ATUM, the triad god from the Delta! He is promoting the worship of Deltan gods over Theban gods.

By year 5 of his reign, A4 severs all links to the old gods, which would have upset the conservative southern Thebans.

By year 9 of his reign, A4 promotes Aten worship and changes his name to Akhenaten. A religious revolution has begun!

For Nefertiti, she strengthens her position by inviting key members of her family to court, especially her father Ay and her brother Smenkhkare. What was her succession plan? Although she knows Moses is a Hebrew, she raises him as her own child, training him to rule. Her plan? It doesn't say, but we get a few clues in the Bible. It appears as if Nefertiti is going to steal the throne. How? She will offer her daughter (divine blood, ½ Deltan, ½ Theban) Merit-aten to Moses in marriage. Thanks to the rule changes of Amenhotep III, a divine daughter can marry someone outside of the royal family. Of course, this would allow:

Pharaoh Moses!

(Unfortunately for Nefertiti, God had other plans for Moses).

CHAPTER FOUR

MO'S BETTER BLUES

So baby "Drew" (Moses=I DREW him out of the water) grew up and lived happily ever after...until he killed a guy.

The details of Moses' life from the age of three months to forty are fairly limited, and initially, seemed problematic for creating a whole chapter. It only took a little prying to discover there were all sorts of intriguing problems and situations that would have faced Pharaoh Akhenaten, Queen Nefertiti, and Prince Drew. Hollywood filled this void with make-believe plots about conflict between Moses and his foster-brother. The timeline for the 18th Dynasty, however, has Ramses coming to power at the age of 16 when Moses is 80, so...not rivals (goo, goo, give me my rattle vs. eh, eh, I need my cane). Also, if it is indeed the court of Akhenaten, then there were no sons anyway...thus, Prince Drew.

Grooming Moses

There are two spots in the Bible that amplify what happened when the Princess "drew" the Hebrew baby from the water. The first verse comes from Luke the Researcher (not a real title).

[Acts 7:20] In which time Moses was born, and was exceeding fair, and nourished up in his father's house three months: [21] And when he was cast out, Pharaoh's daughter took him up, and nourished him for her own son. [22] And Moses was learned in all the wisdom of the Egyptians, and was mighty in words and in deeds.

So, pretty close to what we got in Exodus. Beautiful baby? Check. Three months old? Check. Pharaoh's daughter? Check, but I still think "daughter"-in-law. Took him as her own son? Check. Now, verse 22 is where things get amplified.

Nefertiti did not just use him as an emotional blanket to compensate for her inability to produce a male child for her husband. Luke implies that Moses was educated also. Now, why would you do that? If he was just a human doll, you could keep him dumb, like a court jester. What need did her baby doll have for an education? Especially a slave baby?

If you compare this with any other "daughter" in the 18th dynasty, it really doesn't make a lot of sense. For Nefertiti, it makes a lot of practical sense. She has daughters who are spiritually capable of becoming queen. Thanks to Amenhotep III, a new policy exists that allows royal daughters to marry non-royal men. Moses could marry one of her daughters and...rule?

Remember, she is trying to steal power from Team Thebes and return it to Team Delta. Without a son, her daughters might be forced to marry a Theban and then the control of

Egypt would return to those southern rednecks. Nefertiti does not want this to happen.

Mighty in Words

So not only is Moses an emotional answer to her prayers, but she immediately sees him as a political answer to them as well. According to my Oxford timeline, Nefertiti would become Queen when Moses was five years old. It does appear that Moses stayed with Nefertiti during these formative years, but when Moses turned five, Queen Nefertiti could have lavished him with "all the wisdom of the Egyptians."

What does "all the wisdom" mean? Have you seen the topics about Egypt covered on the *History Channel*? Did the ancient Egyptians understand astronomy? Yep. Did they understand math to build pyramids? Yep? Was history important to the Egyptians? Yep. Did the Egyptians trade with the rest of the world by land and sea? Yep. Did the Egyptians have literature and the arts? Yep. Heck, the Egyptians even invented beer. Moses could have been given all of these wisdoms.

What was Moses' language? Did he speak Hebrew or Egyptian? Ah! Luke says Moses was mighty in "words" and deeds, yet by the time he is 80, Moses balks at God's plan to say "let my people go" because…what? What happened to Moses' training? His gift with "words"? Consider that his native language might have been Egyptian instead of Hebrew.

This could have caused him issues, right?

He lived with Egyptians his first forty years, and then he lived with Midianites the next forty. He went 80 years since he was hanging around Hebrews on a daily basis. Yes, it could have been psychological or physical, but being raised in the Egyptian Education System might have caused this issue.

If Nefertiti wanted to restore a Delta Dynasty, Moses would be her instrument. She was building the perfect prince. Luke implies Moses was mighty in "deed" as well, but we're going to table that for a few minutes. I finished Chapter 3 with a theory on why Nefertiti would have been a spiritual ally for Moses and the Hebrews, and nowhere else in the totality of Egyptian history was there a spiritual upheaval than during the time of Nefertiti's reign.

A Bit about Aten

If Team Delta already had a triad and creation story similar to Elohim and Adam, then evangelizing could have easily happened. Nefertiti did not just pick up the baby, straight-arm Miriam, and run into the palace away from Jochebed (Ex 6:20)—she brought Jochebed to her house and even paid her for nursing Moses. Did Miriam get to come with? Aaron and Amram? It doesn't say. Without an answer or explanation, all I can do is look at what happened in Egypt during the youth of Moses and deduce the answers. Here is a quick timeline:

Moses	What's going on
@ 3 months=	Moses is rescued by Nefertiti
@ five years=	Amenhotep III dies
@ five years=	Amenhotep IV takes the throne.
@ 5-10 years=	Amenhotep promotes the Atum triad
@ 10 years=	A4 changes his name to Akhenaten
@ 14 years=	Akhenaten bans all worship but Aten
@ 22 years=	Akhenaten dies suddenly

Because worship of Aten was abolished and obliterated by later Pharaohs (Horemheb through Ramses the Great), the religion of this time period is only coming to the light in the last century or so. As a result, theories vary wildly. I've seen some that characterize Akhenaten as the precursor of the Antichrist while others credit him for inventing God as a monotheistic entity. Here's what I do know: Ramses hated it. Horemheb hated it. As a result, Nefertiti was hated also. And Egyptian records of Hebrews and Moses? They don't exist. I think the forces of GOOD and EVIL stand on opposite sides during this era.

So what is it?

For 2,000 years of worship, Ra was the predominant sun god in a pantheon of gods. There were already minor gods to explain other aspects of heat also. Yet during this time period, Aten comes out of the blue to become the official state religion during the reign of Akhenaten.

The basic concept of Aten (vs. Ra) is that Aten is light (instead of the sun). In the surviving art, the hands of Aten touch all of creation with little, gentle cupped hands. He has no graven animal images or symbols. Aten is good.

Yup. That's all, folks.

Amenhotep IV could easily have worshiped Ra, Sekhmet, Horus, Khepri, or Atum if he just wanted to worship the sun/light. Instead, he promotes something new. And then he banishes all the old worship. This is a very bold move, even for dudes who think they are deities. Yes, he renames himself after Aten, but most pharaohs already did name variations. He wanted Aten to be worshipped and there were NO OTHER GODS. Monotheism.

Arrogance? Insanity? True believer?

My theory is that Aten MIGHT have been a poor attempt at promoting the Hebrew god. Nefertiti could already have been influenced by the Hebrews while living in Goshen. We saw how open-minded A4/Akhenaten was to her religion over his Theban gods, and if Moses/Miriam/Jochebed had his ear, he could have easily changed his views again. Moses as a ten-year-old preacher is a bit of a reach, but it is possible. So too is Hebrew influence via Moses' family members. Regardless, Akhenaten changes teams, bans other gods, and begins building a new center of worship called Amarna—that's bold!

The name ATEN simply means "disk," and considering the Egyptians were the first to draw something that looked like a halo, there is nothing spooky or sinister about it yet.

A Father-Son Conversation

Let's visualize the conversation of Amenhotep IV for a bit.

A4: "So tell me about your God, Moses."

Moses: "Well, he is the creator and only true god. He created everything."

A4: "How did creation start?"

Moses: Day one...let there be light.

A4: "And what does your God look like?"

Moses: "Not sure. We don't make graven images of him."

A4: "And his name?"

Moses: "In the days before the flood, men invoked His name, but we've been careful and reverent not to use the name since those days. We keep it pretty generic."

A4: "So no proper names like Ra? Osiris? Horus? You do know how important names are to the Egyptian concept of immortality. To convert the others, we're going to need to call the God of Abraham something cool. No proper name?"

Moses: "Nope, but if I ever get an opportunity, I will ask God what he'd like to be called. I'm betting he will have rules about using it, though."

So Amenhotep IV calls his new monotheistic light god...Aten. Decades later, Moses does in fact get a chance to ask God his name. God's response? "I AM WHO I AM." Was God being snarky or serious? Did he dodge the answer or give him a specific title?

Well, let's look at what Moses wrote down.

Yes, Moses did write the Hebrew phrase YHWH, which the Hebrews refused to use with the vowels. What did they say aloud? Adonai. What did the vowels create? Yahweh is the most popular translation. What does it mean? I AM. But Moses, who wrote the first five books of the Bible AFTER this conversation does not use one name. Instead, he uses all sorts of different names ranging from Elohim to El Shaddai. Seriously, you could write a book on all of the name variations and titles used for God in the Bible. Moses asked the question, but the implied answer did not fit the proper name concept.

So using Aten as a word for God is no different than using the English words Almighty, Lord, or Creator.

My misguided point is that while Moses was in the Egyptian Court, the religion of the Egyptians veered dramatically closer to the Biblical God and was then crushed by the same people who wanted to kill Moses. Too Good to Be True! (which is why it all fits for me).

Moses and Merit Sitting in a Tree

So yes, it is just a theory of mine that Nefertiti would have saved Moses so that he could marry one of her biological daughters to secure the throne for Team Delta. It is conjecture that she trained Moses in words and deeds (still more of that later) so that he could be the perfect prince to her daughter. Yet there is a VERY intriguing verse about Moses from the writer (I'm team Barnabas) of *Hebrews*:

> **[Hebrews 11:23] By faith Moses, when he was born, was hid three months of his parents, because they saw he was a proper child; and they were not afraid of the king's commandment. 24 By faith Moses, when he was come to years, refused to be called the son of Pharaoh's daughter; [25] Choosing rather to suffer affliction with the people of God, than to enjoy the pleasures of sin for a season; [26] Esteeming the reproach of Christ greater riches than the treasures in Egypt: for he had respect unto the recompense of the reward. [27] By faith he forsook Egypt, not fearing the wrath of the king: for he endured, as seeing him who is invisible. [28] Through faith he kept the Passover, and the sprinkling of blood, lest he that destroyed the firstborn should touch them. [29] By faith they passed through the Red sea as by dry land: which the Egyptians assaying to do were drowned.**

The writer of *Hebrews* confirms the common beliefs about Moses centuries after his death, so I put the whole thing in there at this point. Depending on your translation, this section has some pretty intriguing phrases. First, it does imply that Moses had faith as a young man. His years of Egyptian education did not brainwash him into idolatry. It even builds on what kind of faith he had by suggesting that he not only was an "OT God" fella, but that he believed in the whole thing, including the promise of the coming Christ. It was because of Christ that Moses refused his Egyptian identity.

But what exactly was he refusing?

Pleasure?

Sin?

Riches?

Being called "son"?

Certainly, it is possible that he just rebelled against his foster family and wanted to be Team Hebrew. But I think he rebelled for a very specific reason: marriage. In researching the timeline for the reign of Akhenaten and Nefertiti, there are some key moments in their history. Now, we've already talked about the religious upheaval they promoted, but there are some minor details happening in the court that have long term impacts.

First, Nefertiti's brother, Smenkhkare (Team Delta) was married to her daughter, Merit-aten. If you ever wondered why we had such specific moral codes written in the book of Leviticus, this is probably your answer. Yes, Uncle Smen married his niece Merit. Ewww!!!!!

At the same time period, another critical event happens: Akhenaten takes on a 2nd wife, Kiya. Now, Queen Nefertiti keeps her crown, and her royal daughters, and her bro/son-in-law Smen, but Akhenaten realizes he needed to take another wife in order to produce a male heir.

What suddenly happened?

Was the heat on from Team Thebes?

After all, Akhenaten's royal sister Mudnodjme had married a non-royal Theban by the name of Horemheb. If Akhenaten died, he would have no legal heir, and the wealth would revert back to his...sister and bro-in-law, Horemheb.

Or was there another reason?

One of the reasons why I advocate Ramses the Great as the pharaoh of Exodus is that everything in the 18th Dynasty seems to match up so well. Here is another instance. How old would Moses have been when this happened?

Seventeen!

Is that what the Hebrews author meant when Moses was "come to years"? It was time to get married. Nefertiti's careful plan was about to save the day. An educated, sophisticated adopted Hebrew son could marry her daughter Merit-Aten and they would have the power to steal the throne away from the Team Thebes. At first, Moses would just be a prince, but when foster dad dies, Moses and Merit could claim the throne of Egypt ahead of Horemheb. Problem solved.

"Thanks, but no thanks..."

WHAT? Imagine the chaos and turmoil Moses would have caused by rejecting this marriage. He would have officially joined the 18th Dynasty...son. He would have become the legal heir of foster dad...rich. He would have married a prin- cess...pleasure (Who he'd grown up with as brother and sister...sin). Why would Moses say no to the nice lady who plucked him from the Nile?

Christ.

Yep, Moses says no on principle.

This leaves Nefertiti scrambling. To help Team Delta stay in power, she takes her own daughter and marries her to her brother. Since she is not producing a male heir, she might have hatched the plan to bring in Kiya (Sara/Hagar). Her handmaiden could give her a son, and then she could make another Moses clone, marry the boy to one of her younger daughters, and bam...Team Delta rules!

The Downfall of Team Delta

Thanks to Moses, it all falls apart quickly. Kiya does have a child, whom they name Tut (yes THAT Tut). Within 5 years of the marriage refusal, Akhenaten dies. The throne passes to Uncle Smen and Merit, but they rule for less than a year. Then the throne is given to the boy king, Tutankhaten (notice the spelling), who is advised by Vizier Ay (Nefertiti's dad). Team Delta is suddenly very weak.

I think it is time for another recap of how old Moses is during these events:

@ 3 months=	Moses is rescued by Nefertiti
@ five years=	Amenhotep III dies
@ five years=	Amenhotep IV takes the throne.
@ 5-10 years=	Amenhotep promotes the Atum triad
@ 10 years=	A4 changes his name to Akhenaten
@ 14 years=	Akhenaten bans all worship but Aten
@ 17 years=	Smenkhkare married Merit-aten
@ 17 years=	Akhenaten IV takes another wife (Kiya)
@ 17 years=	Tut is born that year
@ 17 years=	**Minor military engagements**
@ 22 years=	Akhenaten dies suddenly

@ 22 years=   Smenkhkare becomes pharaoh

@ 23 years   Smenkhkare dies suddenly

@ 23 years   King Tut becomes pharaoh as a boy

Chaotic times in Thebes, huh?

The Sagacious Deeds

Now, there is something I wanted to get back to that was mentioned in:

[Luke 7:22] And Moses was learned in all the wisdom of the Egyptians, and was mighty in words and in deeds.

Words and deeds. What were these deeds that Luke referenced? Biblically, you'd have to pick the stuff from age 80-120, which was a pretty impressive list of deeds. Yet Luke was talking about Moses and his training, so what deeds?

The Hebrew historian Josephus provides all sorts of insight. First, let's talk about Josephus. He is not infallible, but he does give good insight into what folks believed in the era of Christ. He supports a non-Ramses timeline with princess named Thermuthis pulling Moses from the water. He supports a "short" 430 years in Egypt with a direct tree from Amram to Levi.

So Josephus muddies the waters a bit (Nile pun).

According the Josephus, Moses's understanding **"became superior to his age,"** he **"discovered greater quickness of apprehension,"** and they were **"surprised at the beauty of his countenance."**

Later, in Chapter 10, Josephus describes how Moses became a general and was sent to deal with the Ethiopians in the distant lands of Aksum. If this aligns with the "minor military engagements" described during the reign of Akhenaten, then at 17, Moses might have performed his first miracle. Josephus describes how young Moses uses **"a wonderful demonstration of sagacity"** and employs **"stratagem"** to defeat the Ethiopians with "great slaughter."

He not only defeated the invaders, but he pushed them all the way back to their cities, which he besieged. During one of the fights at the city walls, Moses apparently impressed the Ethiopian princess Tharbis, who **"fell deeply in love with him."** Instead of sacking the city, Moses made a marriage alliance with Miss Tharbis, and after accepting surrender, **"consummated this marriage."**

All at the age of 17.

Now, I'm not sure if this tale should happen before or after the rejection of Nefertiti. If it happened before, then it gives him a reason to reject Merit-aten. "Sorry, ma, I got married to Tharbis while I was away." If this happened prior, then he would have returned to Thebes as a hero, beloved by all Egyptians (except for General Horemheb). General Moses could marry Princess Merit as a REWARD for his service.

If it happened AFTER, then he is being punished. He is being thrown to the dogs. General Horemheb and the Thebans could get rid of Moses and weaken Team Delta. Akhenaten and Nefertiti would have been insulted by his rejection and might have wanted him out of their sights. Go to Ethiopia!

Yet, look at how power shifted suddenly. With his marriage alliance to Tharbis, Moses now has two armies. If foster-dad did indeed make him Commander of the Armies of Upper Egypt, then he now also has the power of Ethiopia also. Team Delta and the Hebrews are plentiful in the north, leaving Team Thebes sandwiched in the middle.

Nefertiti would have been pleased.

But Tharbis is a made up story, right?

Moses lives happily ever after with Zipporah, the gal from the well in Midian.

Right?

Unfortunately, there isn't much about Tharbis. Did he have a one-night stand and then forget about her? Did he bring her back? Heck, Moses could have an heir in Aksum!

Strangely, there is a reference to Tharbis in the Bible.

> **[Numbers 12:1] Then Miriam and Aaron spoke against Moses because of the Ethiopian woman whom he had married; for he had married an Ethiopian woman. 2 So they said, "Has the Lord indeed spoken only through Moses? Has He not spoken through us also?" And the Lord heard it. 3 (Now the man Moses was very humble, more than all men who were on the face of the earth.)**

Quick recap. Moses is 81ish here, and we've had the 10 Plagues, the Red Sea, and 10 Commandments by this point. Aaron and Miriam, his Hebrew siblings, are in their late 80s and have spent a year in the wilderness. The people are restless and questioning the leadership of Moses. In their jealousy, Aaron and Miriam bring up a scandal from six decades earlier as proof of Moses's fallibility. It was an old sex scandal. Now, God puts Aaron and Miriam in their place and reconfirms Moses as the righteous authority in the camp.

What does this mean about Tharbis?

It was not a fling? It was a legit marriage? Was Tharbis dead by the time Moses married Zipporah? Only God knew the truth, and Miriam was speaking from a position of ignorance.

Nefertiti vs. Horemheb

Even though Moses did not marry Merit-Aten, he would have remained a powerful man in Thebes when he returned. In a way, he was in the middle of two powerful houses. Yes, the Hebrews were slaves, but there were a million of them along the Nile, especially in the Delta. Now, Moses also has another powerful minority, the Ethiopians.

Team Delta Recap.

So Queen Nefertiti has the most clout, but she has infused the court with her Deltans. Her father Ay was Vizier and her brother Smenkhkare has just married her daughter, Merit-aten. With other daughters, she can further strengthen Team Delta before anything happens to her husband. She is playing the end game.

Team Thebes Recap

General Horemheb is the most powerful person around even though he is not a royal. He did marry Mudnodjme, who was the daughter of Amenhotep III and sister to the current king. Because of her divine blood, he rises to the rank of Commander of the Armies of Lower Egypt, which is large to maintain the Hebrew slaves and fight off any threats from the Middle-East. His southern allies include two military men, Ramses I and Seti I. After biting their tongues for 17 years, Akhenaten dies.

Score Update: Nefertiti 0 Horemheb 1

Horemheb jumped off the page for me. He was unlike any other pharaoh of his day, and his motivations really seemed to match the situation in which Moses found himself when he killed a man. So after one of the most turbulent reigns Egypt had seen in centuries, Akhenaten dies, leaving the future of Egypt in turmoil. For the promoters of Aten, everything is in jeopardy. For Moses, his position as prince and general are in jeopardy. For the Hebrews, who are slaves working for the 18th Dynasty, freedom is in jeopardy. Team Delta vs. Team Thebes is about to begin.

Now, I'm not sure how it happened, but Smenkhkare becomes Pharaoh, and I have to assume it is because he married the divine daughter, Meritaten. Akhenaten's only biological son, Tut, is not even close to being old enough to hold court, so Nefertiti turns to her brother, whom she can trust. He'd been part of the rule of Egypt but was also a Deltan, meaning Nefertiti pulled a bit of a coup. Nefertiti remained Queen Regent while her daughter became Queen and her brother became Pharaoh. With Moses commanding the Armies of Upper Egypt as well as being a Prince of Ethiopia through his marriage with Tharbis, Nefertiti holds all the cards.

Score Update: Nefertiti 1 Horemheb 1

However, Horcmheb is a bit of a sinister fellow, and he begins a Richard III purge of the 18th Dynasty. As a religious and cultural enemy of Akhenaten, many historians speculate Horemheb might have hastened his death. Despite being a middle-aged man, Pharaoh Smenkhkare only rules for a year before he dies.

Score Update: Nefertiti 1 Horemheb 2

By this time, Nefertiti's surrogate son, Tut, is older and is forced to marry his older sister, Ankhesen-aten. Why? She is Team Delta, old enough to manipulate her bro-sband, and a close ally of Nefertiti. Even though Tut was born to a surrogate mother, Kiya, it is Nefertiti who has controlled court since he was alive. Horemheb had a minor win by getting a regent who is both Team Delta and Team Thebes.

Score Update: Nefertiti 1.5 Horemheb 2.5

However, young Tut quickly sides with Team Delta, picking Nefertiti's father, Ay as his vizier. He also continues promotion of Aten and honors his father. During this time period, Moses would have been in his prime, his late 20s and early 30s. Did this warrior-general influence young Tut? Or was Moses far off in Ethiopia or fighting battles on the edge of the Egyptian frontier. Either way, Queen-regent Nefertiti is catching up.

Score Update: Nefertiti 2 Horemheb 2.5

Things were good for the first few years, but by Tut's third year of rule, he began to shift his allegiances toward his general, Horemheb. He changes his name to Tutankhamen, lifts the ban on Amun and the gods of Team Thebes, and returns worship to Thebes instead of Amarna. Tut also has a Theban tax master named Maya, who helps suppress the Hebrew people and the threat posed by Moses. To counter this, Ay remarries a royal daughter to secure his future place.

Score Update: Nefertiti 2 Horemheb 3

When the sickly Tut dies, control of Egypt is once again up in the air. Tut did not produce any heirs, but somehow Nefertiti again manipulates things so that her own father, Ay, the vizier of Egypt, ends up ruling Egypt. At this time, Moses is 32 years old. If he'd given Nefertiti her wish, he would have been Pharaoh with Merit-aten during all this upheaval. Did he remain an active part of the court?

Score Update: Nefertiti 3 Horemheb 3

Despite tying things up, Nefertiti had played her last card. Her father Ay was old and did not produce an heir. He did manage to rule for five years, although historians are unclear if Ay was just a puppet. When Ay does die, Nefertiti and Horemheb came to some sort of truce. It was decided that Tut's widow, who died without an heir, should return as Queen Ankhesen-aten.

This childless widow rule (Deut 25:7-9) is seen in our Bible with the story of Tamar (Gen 38). In the story, Judah is expected to provide a husband for Tamar since she died without a child/son to take care of her. It was a legal obligation for Judah.

For Nefertiti, this is a win because Ahkhesen-aten is her biological daughter. For Horemheb, this is a win because the husband could be a Theban or a stranger who could be neutral. Word is spread throughout the land and neighboring countries that the hand of the Queen could be purchased with a big dowry. As a result, princes from near and far came to Egypt with carts full of treasure to woo Tut's widow.

And then Horemheb kills them all!

Score Update: Nefertiti 3 Horemheb 4

Yep, the mask comes off.

Horemheb is the villain, and he owns it! In killing all the suitors, he fired a warning shot to all the neighboring countries to not mess with Egypt. It also leaves his house wealthy. In this moment, he uses his marriage to Mudnodjme (daughter of AIII/sister of A4) to supersede all those with Deltan blood to produce a pure-blood Theban marriage. Killing the suitors must have been quite the coup, and I'm not sure if Team Delta was impacted. Based on Moses's presence, I think Horemheb only took out the suitors and left Nefertiti and the Deltans alone. He surrounds himself with more Thebans, promoting Ramses (the first) as his Vizier and naming Ramses' son, Seti, as the new Commander of the Armies of Lower Egypt, who can now further oppress the Hebrew workforce as well as the private holdings of Team Delta. Moses might still be Commander of the Armies of Upper Egypt and a Prince of Ethiopia, but only because he is a dangerous foe.

Score Update: Nefertiti 3 Horemheb 5

At 37, Moses has some choices in front of him. Once Horemheb takes control, he immediately begins to implement a very pro-Egyptian, anti-others series of policies. He returns traditional worship and begins to dismantle everything done at Amarna. Although his old wife cannot provide an heir, he places his Theban friends in a position to rule after he is gone. If the Hebrews and Deltans are to continue to worship "God," something needs to be done, and Moses is the last chance for Nefertiti.

Moses Messes Up

So, it's time to go back to the Bible. We've all read the story, but let's look at it in a different light. Moses grew up in Thebes. His Hebrew family lived upriver/south of Thebes, and since being adopted into Team Delta, Nefertiti has kept him either in Thebes or down in Ethiopia. But most of the Hebrews are slaves way up north in the Delta.

> **[Exodus 2:11] And it came to pass in those days, when Moses was grown, that he went out unto his brethren, and looked on their burdens: and he spied an Egyptian smiting an Hebrew, one of his brethren. [12] And he looked this way and that way, and when he saw that there was no man, he slew the Egyptian, and hid him in the sand. [13] And when he went out the second day, behold, two men of the Hebrews strove together: and he said to him that did the wrong, Wherefore smitest thou thy fellow? [14] And he said, Who made thee a prince and a judge over us? intendest thou to kill me, as thou killedst the Egyptian? And Moses feared, and said, Surely this thing is known.**

Unto his brethren? While there certainly were slaves in Thebes working on the Valley of the Kings, most slaves were in the "land of Goshen" working in the brick factories in the muddy Delta, right? What was Moses up to? Why would he make a multi-day, hundreds of miles trip to the Delta?

Moses is about to make a counter-coup.

Think about it. If he could enlist the help of the Hebrew workforce in the Delta, along with his marital allegiances to

Ethiopia, and his unclear military connections with the Army of Upper Egypt, he could raise quite the sedition against a fascist tyrant like Horemheb.

Wow, secret agent man!

Instead of this scene just being an accident, what if it is a plot? He is down in Goshen stoking the fires of a rebellion, kills an Egyptian, and then learns that rumors of it have leaked. The rumor is the threat. Yes, the Hebrews had no reason to rat on Moses, but if they knew General Moses was there, Horemheb's spies might have learned also.

Listen to what Josephus had to say about this time: **"Now the Egyptians, after they had been preserved by Moses, entertained hatred to him, and were eager in compassing their designs against him, as suspecting that he would take occasion, from his good success, to raise a sedition, and bring innovations into Egypt; and told the king that he ought to be slain."**

Sounds like Horemheb, doesn't it?

Yes, Moses would have earned the death penalty. During the reign of Horemheb, it was the death penalty for a foreigner to strike an Egyptian, and Moses did WAY more than that to the taskmaster in Goshen. According to Josephus, after the plot is discovered:

"Moses went away privately; and because the public roads were watched, he took his flight through deserts, and where his enemies could not suspect he would travel, and though he was destitute of food, he went on, and despised that difficulty courageously, and he came to the city Midian, which lay upon the Red Sea."

Not suspect?

Where could Moses run?

Thebes? Nope. Team Delta is almost powerless.

Not Goshen, where the murder most likely took place because that is the territory of General Seti.

Not Nubia/Ethiopia because he'd have to travel through Thebes AND they would look to assassinate him if he went to get help from Tharbis.

He went to Midian, where he could hide.

We'll continue the story of Moses in Chapter Six, but his exile poses an interesting question for me...Why didn't he go back to the Promised Land? Why didn't he go back to Canaan?

CHAPTER FIVE

SON OF A WHAT?

Long ago, back in the book of Genesis, Jacob and sons were pastoral farmers tending their flocks in some of the best real estate on earth. Canaan had mountains and valleys, large lakes and swiftly flowing rivers, and cedar forests that would have made the air a joy to breath. Heck, it was a land that flows with milk and honey.

Canaan rules!

Of course, that was approximately, er…, exactly 430 years ago to the day Moses departed Egypt. 430 years B.E. (before Exodus?), the world experienced a catastrophe on a global scale that forced Jacob and sons to relocate to Egypt, where Joseph had prepared contingencies.

Here is my first question: Why didn't Jacob go back after the seven years of famine ended?

Now, the famine was precisely predicted. We had seven years of plenty followed by seven years of famine. How can you tell it was exactly seven years of famine? Well, conditions must have improved. Famine over.

Canaan is not that far away from Egypt that the weather patterns would have been so dramatically different, leaving you with the answer that A. Egypt was just better, or B. Something was wrong with Canaan.

Of course, a major complication happened when the Hyksos invaders came and turned everybody not Hyksosian (is that a word?) into slaves. When the Hyksos were defeated, those Hebrews alive had been born in Egypt, their home away from home. Yet despite the escalation of tensions between the Thebans and Hebrews, colonies did not flare up in Canaan. Think of the American South prior to the Civil War. Slaves ran away to the north on a regular basis, bringing you the Underground Railroad system. For Southern Slaves, they were willing to leave a bad place to go to a place they didn't even know. For the Hebrew slaves, they were also in a bad place with a God-given paradise waiting for them just a few hundred miles away. Aside from the kind-hearted prostitute Rahab, there were ZERO allies living in Canaan when Joshua rolled in, leaving you with two options again: A. Egypt was better (not!), or B. Something was wrong with Canaan.

Let's talk about life forty years before the Exodus.

Moses has just killed an Egyptian and needs to run away. He can go anywhere, but instead decides to go to Midian, which is just fine. But why didn't he go to Canaan? Moses was a leader and warrior in his prime. He could have gone Samson on the locals, winning a hill, then a valley, then a region, and then the whole territory back in the name of God.

Nope...Midian.

Dramatically, I need to understand the motivations of not only Moses but of every single Hebrew not willing to return to Canaan.

God's Plan for Canaan

This is not just about slavery.

If it was, God could have flipped the tables and given Moses victory in a great civil war, robbing the Thebans of their rule and giving Egypt to the Hebrews. Yet God didn't.

[Exodus 3:4] God called unto him out of the midst of the bush, and said, Moses, Moses. And he said, Here am I. [5] And he said, Draw not nigh hither: put off thy shoes from off thy feet, for the place whereon thou standest is holy ground. [6] Moreover he said, I am the God of thy father, the God of Abraham, the God of Isaac, and the God of Jacob. And Moses hid his face; for he was afraid to look upon God.

[7] And the LORD said, I have surely seen the affliction of my people which are in Egypt, and have heard their cry by reason of their taskmasters; for I know their sorrows; [8] And I am come down to deliver them out of the hand of the Egyptians, and to bring them up out of that land unto a good land and a large, unto a land flowing with milk and honey; unto the place of the Canaanites, and the Hittites, and the Amorites, and the Perizzites, and the Hivites, and the Jebusites. [9] Now therefore, behold, the cry of the children of Israel is come unto me: and I have also seen the oppression wherewith the Egyptians oppress them.

[10] Come now therefore, and I will send thee unto Pharaoh, that thou mayest bring forth my people the children of Israel out of Egypt. [11] And Moses said unto God, Who am I, that I

should go unto Pharaoh, and that I should bring forth the children of Israel out of Egypt? [12] And he said, Certainly I will be with thee; and this shall be a token unto thee, that I have sent thee: When thou hast brought forth the people out of Egypt, ye shall serve God upon this mountain.

God wanted them to go to Canaan. It was his plan. Granted, it took another 40+ years before it happened, but it was already a land that flowed with milk and honey. It should have been a huge draw, but it wasn't. So what was wrong?

The Problem with Paradise

We can see the answer with the report of the Hebrew spies.

[Numbers 13:21] So they went up, and searched the land from the wilderness of Zin unto Rehob, as men come to Hamath. [22] And they ascended by the south, and came unto Hebron; where Ahiman, Sheshai, and Talmai, the children of Anak, were. (Now Hebron was built seven years before Zoan in Egypt.) [23] And they came unto the brook of Eshcol, and cut down from thence a branch with one cluster of grapes, and they bare it between two upon a staff; and they brought of the pomegranates, and of the figs. [24] The place was called the brook Eshcol, because of the cluster of grapes which the children of Israel cut down from thence. [25] And they returned from searching of the land after forty days. [2]6 And they went and came to Moses, and to Aaron, and to all the congregation of the children of Israel, unto the wilderness of Paran, to Kadesh; and brought back word unto them, and unto all the congregation, and shewed them the fruit of the land. [27] And they told him, and said, We came unto the land whither thou sentest us, and surely it floweth with milk

and honey; and this is the fruit of it. [28] Nevertheless the people be strong that dwell in the land, and the cities are walled, and very great: and moreover we saw the children of Anak there. [29] The Amalekites dwell in the land of the south: and the Hittites, and the Jebusites, and the Amorites, dwell in the mountains: and the Canaanites dwell by the sea, and by the coast of Jordan.

[30] And Caleb stilled the people before Moses, and said, Let us go up at once, and possess it; for we are well able to overcome it. 31 But the men that went up with him said, We be not able to go up against the people; for they are stronger than we. [32] And they brought up an evil report of the land which they had searched unto the children of Israel, saying, The land, through which we have gone to search it, is a land that eateth up the inhabitants thereof; and all the people that we saw in it are men of a great stature. [33] And there we saw the giants, the sons of Anak, which come of the giants: and we were in our own sight as grasshoppers, and so we were in their sight.

So there is quite a bit to unpack in that section. Remember that Moses picked the biggest, bravest man from the twelve tribes, so these 12 spies are the elite warriors from all of Israel and not just some scrubs. Upon returning, ten of twelve are terrified of what they saw, and despite having the God of the 10 Plagues, the Crossing of the Red Sea, and the Ark of the Covenant, they do NOT think it is a fight they can win.

What?!?!

First, they make a reference to the "Children of Anak" as if we know who the heck Anak is, which we don't. It's bad. Very bad, but we'll just ignore it and look at the other facts.

Canaan has gone from fertile pastures to a land that is fortified and strong, which is a tad anachronistic compared to ancient Egypt, where we do have cool pyramids and temples but no walled fortresses. What did the people of Canaan need the tall walls for?

It makes a quick reference to the **"Amalekites, Hittites, Jebusites, and Amorites"** as if listing off English, French, Spanish, and Swedish. While the Hittites have historical reference, the other two (Jebusites and Amorites) have few non-Biblical references, and the Amalekites have a downright bizarre connotation, which we'll talk about in Chapter Ten.

The walls are not the only problem, and the spies describe the Canaanites as being "stronger than we," which is surprising considering these are slaves of the field and probably pretty ripped after generations of slave labor. But they are big.

Next, we have this juicy nugget: eating. Depending on your translation, this is personification of the land by saying that the LAND eats its inhabitants, which is paradoxical when you remember that the LAND is flowing with milk and honey. So if the general environment is paradise, what is doing the eating? Eating your inhabitants? If the inhabitants are the Canaanites, then who or what is eating them? Is this cannibalism? Or is it worse?

The third reason for the spies FREAKING OUT builds slowly. Again, twelve warriors go to Canaan and suddenly develop a massive inferiority complex. They claim that the inhabitants are "strong," and "men of great stature" before finally coming out and saying they felt like "grasshoppers" compared to them. Hyperbole? At its minimal, they are expressing that they can't win because the DUDES ARE BIG. This is coming from an army of

600,000 bricklayers with an Ark of the Covenant. They are intimidated.

Unfortunately, the BIG metaphor has even more clues once you start peeling it apart. Again, leaving Anak alone, there is another coded reference that should be jaw dropping: Nephilim. Didn't see that? Well, my King James translation is a bit underwhelming in literal translation. Instead of using the word Nephilim, they jump the gun and use the word GIANTS, which I get. The spies were saying they saw big guys, and then connected it to the ancient legend of the Nephilim from Genesis 6, which was (See Chapter 1) approximately 1,400 years earlier.

Yeah, we saw *those* guys!

Facing Your Giants

Okay, I get that giants are pretty fantastical and a bit embarrassing to modern Christians. Back in the 1600s, the KJV writers just dropped giants right on the page whereas modern translations will put the old Hebrew word Nephilim on the page and let the reader deal with the fantasy connotations. Heck the KJV left the word UNICORN in the Bible (Rhino or real?). Bringing up Fallen Angels is no less fantastical than giants, but I get how this could give modern Christians pause. So we'll deal with the elephant in the room.

Option A: Flat Lies. Yes, the spies could have been fibbing. For whatever reason, the spies did not want to reclaim the homeland and wanted to either stay in the wilderness until the manna ran out or to go back to Egypt. To accomplish this, they made up a story about cannibal giants to freak out the Hebrews. If so, it worked. But why did Joshua and Caleb not only agree to the lie but then try to convince the people that they could beat the giants? It would have been easier to say "Not true. Regular dudes. We can kill them all."

Option B: Hyperbole. Okay, so if Joshua was short at five-foot tall, and a Hebrew grasshopper was really big at five inches tall, then these giants would have been about fifty feet tall. Fee, fi, fo, fum! They were big but thanks to hyperbole they were stretching the truth a bit. Big dudes! Really big dudes! We felt like Mugsy Bogues taking on Shaquille O'Neal. Grasshoppers!

Option C: Genetic Superiority. On the isolated continent of North America, there was a Native American tribe living in the Midwest known as the Osage, who painter George Catlin described as being the "tallest race of men in North America." This isolated tribe averaged six and a half to seven feet tall and caused all their neighbors to greatly fear them. Is that what Joshua and Caleb saw? A genetically superior race that was just bigger and better than anything else in the region? Remember (conspiracy theory alert) that the Hyksos people left Egypt in defeat and might have settled in empty Canaan. If these guys are the Hyksos 2.0, then remember that some theorists believe the Hyksos migration connected to Aryan migrations, which is where Hitler would have claimed "Canaanites? Nein...Atlantcans!" (But Hitler was nuts).

While we're being nutty, consider the Big Foot/Grendel Idea. What if these folks in Canaan were the last of some ancient race? As an English teacher, I teach **Beowulf**, which has Grendel described as the last of an ogre race descended from Cain. I suppose you could throw in legends of Big Foot or the Yeti also, yet you still have to account for the Biblical flood, so don't get too carried away.

Option D: Metaphors for Evil. It is all poetry. The size of the man is equal to the amount of evil in his heart. So the Canaanites were not physically larger but just really, really nasty people. We are too nice and they are big bullies. How can we defeat such meanies?

Option E: Supernatural Byproducts. God is once again going to get himself directly involved because giants are not part of his natural plan. As Moses writes (Ah, he did write Genesis too), the Fallen Angels caused problems both before the flood and after the flood. All flesh was killed in the flood, which meant all of the giants before the flood died. So what brought them back? The Fallen Angels, who were NOT flesh and blood but could still create/modify life (ew), survived the flood and are once again about to be spanked by the Creator for being bad.

If you look at the actual Hebrew word rather than the correct but ill-timed connotation, the spies saw FALLEN ANGELS (the daddies) as well as the giants (the abominable kids). While a well-placed spear through the eye should be able to take out a giant, how do you fight a fallen angel? This would freak out the bravest hero!

Meet Anak

Unfortunately, there is not much known about the reference that the spies make. It seems as though the Hebrews knew about Anak but that we've lost much of the meaning in the years since. "**[33] And there we saw** the giants, the sons of Anak, **which come of** the giants: **and we were in our own sight** as grasshoppers, **and so we were in their sight."** Well, it seems as if Anak is either the descendant of fallen angels, and thus a giant, OR he is the fallen angel and his children are the giants. Either way, Anak caused the jaws to drop. He is the reason the spies assume they will lose.

The Hebrew word *Anak* apparently has a few different options. First, it means giant, which from this context, makes sense. It also has the connotation for neck or necklace. Either the "long necks" or "neck chains" is a common interpretation.

But here, the spies claim to see Anak.

Problem: He's really old.

There isn't a nice genealogy chart for Anak, so I'll have to piece this together.

> **[Joshua 15:13] And unto Caleb the son of Jephunneh he gave a part among the children of Judah, according to the commandment of the LORD to Joshua, even the city of Arba the father of Anak, which city is Hebron. [14]And Caleb drove thence the three sons of Anak, Sheshai, and Ahiman, and Talmai, the children of Anak.**

So Anak had kids and also had a father, Arba. Let's track down lines about Arba.

> **[Joshua 14:15]: And the name of Hebron before was Kirjatharba; which Arba was a great man among the Anakims. And the land had rest from war.**

So Arba had a place named after him, let's track down Kirjatharba.

> **[Genesis 23:2] And Sarah died in Kirjatharba; the same is Hebron in the land of Canaan: and Abraham came to mourn for Sarah, and to weep for her.**

Sara? Abraham and Sara. Kirjatharba was already a place when Sara was old. Wait a second! The B.C. and Anno Mundi dates will be a little confusing, but keeping it approximate, Sara died several hundred years prior to the spies seeing Anak. If Arba was alive or predated Sara, then how old is Anak?

Just as Arba and Kirjatharba are referenced numerous times, so too are the Anakim, the descendants of Anak. By the time Joshua is done cleaning up Canaan, they are all gone, but there is a very curious connection back to Genesis that I'd like to show.

[Deut 2:10]: The Emims dwelt therein in times past, a people great, and many, and tall, as the Anakims; [11] Which also were accounted giants, as the Anakims; but the Moabites call them Emims. [12] The Horims also dwelt in Seir beforetime; but the children of Esau succeeded them, when they had destroyed them from before them, and dwelt in their stead;

Translation: Anakim=giants=Emim

Before we chase down the Emim, I need to note that the KJV jumped the gun and once again slapped in the word giant. However, the Hebrew word is rephaim, which does have GIANT connotation, just like Nephilim. REPHAIM will lead us to some other cool verses also. This is a big can of worms the spies just opened up.

Before I go down the rabbit hole, let's finish up with Anak. There seems to be three generations of Anakim yet they are BIG trouble for the spies. As a mythology fan, I have a stray thought. In Babylonian mythology, there was something called the Igigi. The Igigi were ten ruling gods (or fallen angels) who are described in the Epic of Gilgamesh (flood lore) as siring children.

Their children were giants who helped build the Tower of Babel and other impressive works right after the flood. Their name...the Annunaki.

Anakim=Annunaki?

I know it is a stretch, but what if the legends overlapped. If Arba was a fallen angel (or Igigi), then his child would have been Anak, a giant (or Annunaki). The Hebrew spies would have seen living legends right out of the Epic of Gilgamesh and the pre-flood world.

Speaking of preflood world, let's go there next.

Old School Giants

I'm going to split hairs now. The Hebrew word Nephilim means "the fallen ones." Based on all the Hebrew legends and lore surrounding this section of Genesis, I'm in the camp that believes this to be the Fallen Angels. When I read Genesis 6, here is how I read it:

> **Genesis 6:4: The giants** (Nephilim=the Fallen angels) **were on the earth** (preflood) **in those days** (preflood) **and afterward** (um...Moses's life) **when the Sons of God** (fallen angels) **came into the daughters of men** (human women) **and bore children** (the genetic giants) **to them. These were the mighty men** (gibbor=giants) **who were of old** (legends), **men of renown** (still talking about them centuries later).

There are a lot of factors for God destroying the earth in 1656 anno mundi. Wickedness...? Lots! This is the generalization given, but it is still hard for me to fathom such an evil world when compared to the violence and evil of...1900-1980. Look at how many people died under Hitler, Stalin, Pol Pot, etc., etc. Genocide by the millions. So how bad was life in 1656 AM? Yet there are other theories for God putting Noah on the Ark. Population control? Cosmic catastrophe? Ecological preservation?

But right in the middle of Genesis 6 is the strange account of the Nephilim. It's in the heart of the explanation of wickedness. Centuries later, it is in the heart of the Exodus story. So what's going on?

Using those words given in Genesis, the literal defense of giants is not very strong. Ignoring the word Nephilim, some folks argue that "sons of god" can mean the line of Seth and the "daughters of men" mean the line of Cain.

Sure.

Now I need an explanation on how the line of Cain survived the flood. Another Ark? There are a lot of other Biblical passages that seem to support the Fallen Angels>Giants theory.

First, Job 1:6 introduces the "sons of god" along with Satan presenting themselves before God and then later in Job 38:7 connects "sons of god" with the "morning stars" who sang together at the beginning of creation. Job is a pretty old book of the Bible, so I think this is what Moses meant when establishing his "sons of god" line.

Also in Genesis 6, you see the word "gibbor," which King David later uses (2 Samuel 23) as a nickname for his crew of killers. What did the Gibbor kill? Giants. There are a bunch of other "gibbor" uses, although not always in the context of giants, but quite often in the context of BIG EVIL.

The curious turn for my investigation into giants came when I read the Book of Jude, verse 6:

[Jude 6]: And the angels which kept not their first estate, but left their own habitation, he hath reserved in everlasting chains under darkness unto the judgment of the great day.

I got curious. When did God lock up angels? What did they do? They "left" their estate? There isn't much from Jude to explain this reference, but he went and stepped in something stickier a few verses later when he said in verse:

[Jude 14]: And Enoch also, the seventh from Adam, prophesied of these, saying, Behold, the Lord cometh with ten thousands of his saints,

Enoch said what? See, the problem is...Enoch did not speak in the Book of Genesis, so I quickly went to my footnotes to see what is going on. Yep, there is a **Book of Enoch.** Now, there are a ton of obvious reasons why this apocryphal book is not in our Bible. We do not even know if the "modern" discovery of the ancient text is the same as the text Jude knew way back in the 1st century. Yes, they found the same verse, but 99% of the rest could be maliciously wrong.

Even though the **Book of Enoch** is not scripturally sound, it does provide context and juxtaposition. So let's take a look at what Jude was referencing.

First, it clearly expands on Genesis 6 by explaining that there were indeed fallen angels who reproduced with human women (no scientific details given). Their children were horrible giants with references to being 300 feet tall. Their nicknames were either translated as "biters" or "bastards." Either is bad. These giants devoured everything in their path, and as a result, the flood helped eliminate them and gave humans a new fighting chance on Earth 2.0.

Giggle, giggle. 300 foot giants?

There are some LOL moments but also some very intriguing concepts dropped in this ancient text, WHICH was discovered in Ethiopia. Ethiopia...Land of Tharbis. Queen of Sheba. It's like Disney Land to Israel's Disney World.

> **[Enoch 15v8]: "Now the giants, who have been born of spirit and flesh, shall be called upon earth evil spirits, and on earth shall be their habitation. Evil spirits shall proceed from their flesh, because they were created from above; from the holy Watchers was their beginning and primary foundation. Evil spirits shall they be upon earth, and spirits of the wicked shall they be called. The habitations of the spirits of heaven shall be in heaven; but upon earth shall be the habitation of terrestrial spirits, who are born on the earth. The spirits of the giants shall be like clouds."**

Demons? So a Fallen Angel creates an abomination, and upon death, it has no place in heaven or hell, so it lingers upon the earth as a...cloud. Think of the demon-possessed man Jesus met on the Sea of Galilee. Legion. Why? Because they were many. Now, why would a once proud angel want to debase itself by possessing a human. A former giant, however, born flesh and now eternally spirit...they would want back in flesh. Remember their fear of the abyss? Perhaps that is what Jude references with the "everlasting chains of darkness." Daddy is in prison. Please don't send me there. So Jesus cast them into a herd of pigs and...cliff.

Clouds? This is where the rabbit hole went even deeper. Let's look back at some of those names mentioned by Joshua and Moses.

Nephilim	=	"the fallen"
Anakim	=	long necked/giant
Emim	=	"frighteners"/giant
Zamzummim	=	"mumblers"/giant
Rephaim	=	"shades/spirits of the dead"

I find it interesting that in this "six degrees of separation" that a dead giant turns into a cloud, and in the text involving giants, the Hebrew word "rephaim" is still used in the era of Moses and Joshua.

Now, I could go on for several more pages about the giants in the Old Testament, so I'll just let you look things up and investigate for yourself.

Genesis 6	=	Nephilim/Gibbor
Genesis 10v8	=	Nimrod was a gibbor
Genesis 14v5	=	Kings subduing Emim/Rephaim
Genesis 15	=	Lot/"land of rephaim"/Moab
Num. 13v28	=	Anakim/Nephilim
Deut 2v9-11	=	Emim/Anakim/Rephaim/Moab
Deut 3	=	King Og is a giant
Deut 9v1-3	=	Burning fire kills most giants
Josh 11v21	=	Joshua kills the rest/King Og
1 Chron 20	=	Giants have six fingers/toes
1 Samuel	=	Goliath

If you like EPIC, it is a fun study. Before I get back to Moses and the Hebrews, I just like to offer a theory. When Genesis 6 claimed the Nephilim were on the earth before the flood and also after the flood, it implies that all the giants died. Did the dead giants become demons or did the flood wipe them away.

Regardless, there were again giants after the flood. Meaning the text of Genesis claiming "all flesh died" was wrong, OR the Fallen Angels did not count/die.

Remember Enoch and Jude? In the ancient tale, right before the flood, angels came and destroyed the giants and then threw the fornicating angels in a pit. Now does Jude and "Legion" make sense? However, just as Satan escaped judgment, I believe other fallen angels escaped the abyss punishment. If fallen angels existed after the flood, they would either be bowed and sheepish after seeing what happened to their work/children OR they would be vengeful. What do we see in the Bible?

Nimrod...just two generations after the flood.

Not sure if he is a giant or a giant hunter, so let's look elsewhere.

Abram and Lot. The rescue of Lot overshadows the war going on. The war? Apparently, a coalition of kings went to deal with the Emim and Rephaim. Afterwards, the coalition broke up and they turned on each other, with Lot as collateral damage.

That was just a few hundred years after the flood.

And dealt with by humans.

A thousand years after the flood, Canaan is infested by giants. It will take Moses, Joshua, the Ark of the Covenant, 600K warriors, and a pillar of fire to restore the land of milk and honey, only to be finished a few hundred years later by King David and his Giant Hunters.

So what happened?

Before I deal with our prime suspects, let's look at the ending.

[Revelation 9:13] And the sixth angel sounded, and I heard a voice from the four horns of the golden altar which is before

God, [14] Saying to the sixth angel which had the trumpet, <u>Loose the four angels</u> which are bound in the great river Euphrates. [15] And the four angels were loosed, which were prepared for an hour, and a day, and a month, and a year, for to slay the third part of men. [16] And the number of the army of the horsemen were <u>two hundred thousand thousand</u>: and I heard the number of them. [17] And thus I saw the horses in the vision, and them that sat on them, having breastplates of fire, and of jacinth, and brimstone: and the heads of the horses were as the heads of lions; and out of their mouths issued fire and smoke and brimstone. [18] By these three was the third part of men killed, by the fire, and by the smoke, and by the brimstone, which issued out of their mouths. [19] For their power is in their mouth, and in their tails: for their tails were like unto serpents, and had heads, and with them they do hurt.

Spooky stuff, but who are those four angels? Where did they get their weirdo army?

Again, this is NOT YET judgment day, so these are not the angels of Jude. So where did these guys come from? What did they do to get locked up? Why such a terrestrial prison? Iraq, seriously? I have no answers, but I do have a theory.

Bad Angel A   =Arba...father of the Long-Neckers.
Bad Angel B   =The Emim...the Frighteners.
Bad Angel C   =The Zamzummim...the Mumblers
Bad Angel D   =Not sure. Horites? Rephaim?

Four angels. Four types of giants. While there were certainly real Canaanites of normal size, outside of the protective walls, four types of giants roamed the woods and mountains of Israel, and God needed a clean up plan less dramatic than a global flood.

So who is to blame?

The Usual Suspects

I propose...the Hyksos. A few centuries before Moses' birth, the Egyptian coalition crushed the foreign kings in a battle in the Sinai peninsula. Unless it was the greatest battle ever, there were survivors. I speculate that the survivors settled in the Holy Land, just beyond the reach of Egypt. I've already established that I believe the Hyksos people serve epically dark deities, and after a massive loss, where would they turn?

New gods?

These gods could be dressed up as Baal and Anath, El and Asherah, or they could have had names lost to us. Ramses the Great seemed to recognize the power of these Canaanite gods when he named his daughter after Anath.

Moses? He steered clear of his ancestral homelands when he was on the run.

The Hebrews? They chose to stay in Egypt, both free and slave, rather than go back to Canaan.

So the folks in this time knew something was very, very wrong with Canaan.

And God had a plan to fix it, but first, he needed to get Moses ready.

CHAPTER SIX

CAPTAIN CAVEMAN

We left off with Moses, at the age of forty, going into exile. According to Exodus 2, Moses settled in the Land of Midian, which most scholars place in the northwest corner of the Arabian Peninsula, along the eastern shore of the Red Sea. Even by the 18th Dynasty, the Sinai Peninsula had been utilized by the Egyptians for mining precious jewels, so Moses knew he would have bumped into Egyptian workers. Remember, Horemheb would have seen him as a threat as well as a criminal, so assassins seem par for the course. Knowing this, Moses chose to go to a land of nomads, cut off from society.

Jewish historian Josephus adds some interesting details to the tale. In his account, there was clear animosity between Moses and Pharaoh (Horemheb), so when Moses left Thebes to visit the land of Goshen, his purpose was to "raise a sedition" and "bring innovations into Egypt." In other words, after destroying the Deltan Dynasty, Pharaoh (Horemheb) worried that Moses would scheme to have the Ethiopians and Hebrews rise up against him. So Pharaoh (Horemheb) was "envious" of Moses and plotted to kill him.

Josephus makes no mention of Moses murdering an Egyptian worker, but instead, Moses learns he is about to be assassinated, so he went "where his enemies could not suspect he would travel."

Midian.

Josephus does have the story of the well, and in the familiarity of the shared story, I almost missed a couple very cool details. First, Midian is described as the Land of "Keturah," and is clearly described as being upon the Red Sea. But when introducing Zipporah and the sisters, he describes the scene by saying what they were doing was "customary and very familiar for women to do in the country of the Troglodytes."

Huh?

Sock it to me, Moses

Growing up in the 20th Century, I had the social context of Neanderthals, *2001: A Space Odyssey*, the Jimmy Castor Bunch's "Troglodytes," a band called the Troggs, and a club wielding furball on Saturday morning cartoons, but the ancient definition of a "caveman" is far different than the modern context.

Two thousand years ago, historians wrote about a "real" group of people, which they called the Troglodytae. Trogle is the root for the word cave, and dytes is a word that means divers—together, they were the cave divers. Now, based on description and chronology, these cave-divers are not the same as those folks who decorated a few caves with animal graffiti. But these Troglodytes are still quite fascinating.

First, they are not creatures of mythology. In fact, they are referenced by Pliny, Stabo, Josephus, Tacitus, Herodotus, Agatharchides, Diodorus, and Siculus the same way they referenced any other legitimate foreign people. Herodotus gives some description, claiming they were the swiftest runners known, spoke a unique language that no one else understood, and they ate serpents.

Cool, huh?

In the Herodotus account, written after Moses but before Christ, the Troglodytes were nearly extinct, "hunted by the Garamantes people," which meant the Troglodytes people might have existed in northern Africa near Libya.

Strabo clouds things even further when he describes the Troglodytae as being people that lived in the caves of Europe and Asia. Not only is that a large and ambiguous range, but it also gives us three continents of existence.

Josephus's account connects the Troglodytes to the subcontinent of the Middle East, which means this obscure tribe was either the most nomadarific of all nomad tribes or there was something more substantial to them.

In Genesis 25, we get a relatively obscure passage describing how Abraham gets himself a new wife after Sarah dies. We all know how Ishmael became the father of a mighty nation that later became Islam, and how Isaac became the father of a mighty nation that later became Israel and the Jews, but it turns out Abraham has a third branch on his family tree.

[Genesis 25:1] Now Abraham had taken another wife, named Keturah, [2] and she bore him Zimran, Jokshan, Medan, Midian, Ishbak, and Shuah. [3] Jokshan was the father of Sheba and Dedan. And the sons of Dedan were the Asshurites, the Letushites, and the Leummites. [4] The sons of Midian were Ephah, Epher, Hanoch, Abida, and Eldaah. All these were descendants of Keturah.

So Keturah gives him six sons, one of which is named Midian, who gives Abraham five grandsons. And we don't hear from them for almost six centuries. We don't know how Joseph's Cataclysm affected them, nor do we know what happened historically. If 70 Hebrews became 600,000 in the course of 430 years, the full strength of Keturah's nation could also be impressive.

I found a few nuggets in the line of Keturah. Epher, who is a grandson and son of Midian, reportedly left home and invaded Libya, which explains why the Garamantes people were still trying to wipe them out a thousand years later. Epher is also the root for the word Africa (according to the internet), with the word *ifri* becoming Africa while also referencing the fact that Epher was a cave-dweller. Also remember that the Ethiopian version of the Genesis story has Adam and Eve living in the Cave of Treasures upon the Holy Mountain of God.

I'd really love to understand more about the Troglodytes because it appears as if the only thing uniting them is religion and language.

Religion?

Remember when Moses saves the girls at the well, they take Moses to their father, Jethro (also called Reuel), who is already described as a priest (kohen) of Midian. Remember, the Hebrews do not even have an official priestly order. They will in about 40 years with the establishment of the Levites, but at the time of the well, it doesn't exist yet. Nor do any Levitical laws. Yet Jethro shows up out of the blue and is already a priest.

I know this is speculation, but wouldn't it be cool if all the Troglodytes spread across the world were a religious order. Think about it…in the legend of the Holy Mountain of God (Adam and Eve's second home), they lived in a cave. Mount Horeb has a cave. What if they were like monks that spread out (fruitful and multiplying) across the world, still spoke the pre-Babel language, and were just shepherds for wayward travelers—like the Templars without all the occult baggage.

Boot Camp

Even though we don't know HOW Jethro had become a priest, we do know that Moses stays in Midian for the next four decades. Moses returns to Egypt at the age of 80, married and with children.

> **[Exodus 2:15] Now when Pharaoh heard this thing, he sought to slay Moses. But Moses fled from the face of Pharaoh, and dwelt in the land of Midian: and he sat down by a well. [16] Now the priest of Midian had seven daughters: and they came and drew water, and filled the troughs to water their father's flock. [17] And the shepherds came and drove them away: but Moses stood up and helped them, and watered their flock. [18] And when they came to Reuel their father, he said, How is it that ye are come so soon to day? [19] And they said, An Egyptian delivered us out of the hand of the shepherds, and also drew water enough for us, and watered the flock. [20] And he said unto his daughters, And where is he? why is it that ye**

have left the man? call him, that he may eat bread. [21] And Moses was content to dwell with the man: and he gave Moses Zipporah his daughter. [22] And she bare him a son, and he called his name Gershom: for he said, I have been a stranger in a strange land.

And he lived happily ever after...almost.

My assumption used to be that Jethro was older than Moses, but you need to remember that Moses returns to him following the crossing of the Red Sea, so he can't be too much older than Moses at this point.

Another strange thing that can be missed here is the pace of the marriage. Looking at Exodus 2:21, it seems as if Jethro rewards Moses with a spare daughter, but in 4:21, we have a strange scene involving Zipporah circumcising her sons.

Wait! How old were her sons?

Circumcising anyone beyond the age of newborn seems a bit rough, but snipping a man at the age of 37 would be very uncomfortable for everybody. Plus, only dependent children would need to accompany mom and dad back to Egypt. Grown children over the age of ten would just stay with Jethro. Little kids would need their mother. The sons of Moses are young.

But that makes a strange point.

Moses did not have a child for three decades? How long did he wait to marry Zipporah then? Ah, so the timeline found in verse 21 might be a bit compressed, which I like.

The reason why I like this is because Moses needs some spiritual training. Thanks to the education provided by Nefertiti, he has the capacity to lead a nation, but with Jethro, he has an old-school priest who can teach him the mysteries of the faith. Jethro the Troglodyte does not just have *any* territory either...he has the Holy Mountain of God, Mt. Horeb, Mt. Sinai. It almost seems as if Jethro was looking for Moses.

Later, after the divine battle takes place, Jethro greets Moses and the two share a moment.

[Exodus 18:9] And Jethro rejoiced over all the good things the LORD had done for Israel

This guy is a friend and ally. Moses not only shares the gospel, but he leaves his wife and kids with Jethro. His reasons are never clearly stated. It makes sense that Moses would not want his bloodline worshipped as kings after his death. Or…it could be something for Grandpa Reuel. What if Gershom and Eliezer also became Troglodyte priests? How cool would that be?

Coincidentally, the Druze religion claims that Jethro is their great patriarch. Although I wish this religion was some unmolested, ancient version unchanged by man since the days of the Troglodytes, this is not the case. It is neither Judaism no Islam, with a few other concepts thrown in. It is still active yet minimal, but what I like about it is that it does show that the priesthood did not stop with Jethro. It continued. And somewhere, the descendants of Moses are out there.

Changes in Thebes

So after spending years 40-80 in Midian, Moses is stolen out of exile to finally fulfill his destiny.

[Exodus 2:23] After a long time, the king of Egypt died. The Israelites groaned and cried out under their burden of slavery, and their cry for deliverance from bondage ascended to God.

[24] So God heard their groaning, and He remembered His covenant with Abraham, Isaac, and Jacob. [25] God saw the Israelites and took notice.

So what had happened in Egypt during that time?

I assume for the first few years, Horemheb continued to unsuccessfully search for Moses. He would have asked his henchmen to search. It probably consumed him. Now, one of the main reasons I picked the Ramses Theory is that the threat spans forty years. Yes, there were other Pharaohs that ruled for a long time. Tuthmosis III ruled for 54 years, which is almost too long whereas others ruled for just a few short years before dying and passing the torch.

Horemheb takes over when Moses is the right age, rules for a long time, yet passes his throne to his henchmen rather than his heir. When Moses was 40, Horemheb was in his prime, with Vizier Ramses I and General Seti at his side. The "new" Pharaoh of the 10 plagues was not born yet.

Ramses the First/(Grandpa)'s reign is so brief some question if he ruled at all. His son, Seti (Sethos) takes over afterwards, but having been a rival of Moses, God does not recall his champion. Heck, he is named after the God of Evil, Seth. Pharaoh Seti rules for about 14 of the 40 years, and upon his death, God gives Moses the "all clear."

The "new" Pharaoh?

That would be Ramses II, at the ripe age of 16.

He never met Moses.

He most likely never heard of Moses, since the records were undoubtedly erased by Team Thebes over the past four decades.

Bush or Angel?

So Moses goes back. There are a few nuggets I'd like to talk about in his commission and his trek back.

> [Exodus 3:1] Meanwhile, Moses was shepherding the flock of his father-in-law Jethro, the priest of Midian. He led the flock to the far side of the wilderness and came to Horeb, the mountain of God. [2] There the angel of the LORD appeared to him in a blazing fire from within a bush. Moses saw the bush ablaze with fire, but it was not consumed. [3] So Moses thought, "I must go over and see this marvelous sight. Why is the bush not burning up?"
>
> [4] When the LORD saw that he had gone over to look, God called out to him from within the bush, "Moses, Moses!"
> "Here I am," he answered.
>
> [5] "Do not come any closer," God said. "Take off your sandals, for the place where you are standing is holy ground."
>
> [6] Then He said, "I am the God of your father, the God of Abraham, the God of Isaac, and the God of Jacob."
> At this, Moses hid his face, for he was afraid to look at God.
>
> [7] The LORD said, "I have indeed seen the affliction of My people in Egypt. I have heard them crying out because of their oppressors, and I am aware of their sufferings. [8] I have come down to rescue them from the hand of the Egyptians and to bring them up out of that land to a good and spacious land, a land flowing with milk and honey—the home of the Canaanites, Hittites, Amorites, Perizzites, Hivites, and Jebusites.
>
> [9] And now the cry of the Israelites has reached Me, and I have seen how severely the Egyptians are oppressing them.
>
> [10] Therefore, go! I am sending you to Pharaoh to bring My people, the Israelites, out of Egypt."

[11] But Moses asked God, "Who am I, that I should go to Pharaoh and bring the Israelites out of Egypt?"

[12] "I will surely be with you," God said, "and this will be the sign to you that I have sent you: When you have brought the people out of Egypt, all of you will worship God on this mountain."

[13] Then Moses asked God, "Suppose I go to the Israelites and say to them, 'The God of your fathers has sent me to you,' and they ask me, 'What is His name?' What should I tell them?"

[14] God said to Moses, "I AM WHO I AM. This is what you are to say to the Israelites: 'I AM has sent me to you.'"

[15] God also told Moses, "Say to the Israelites, 'The LORD, the God of your fathers—the God of Abraham, the God of Isaac, and the God of Jacob—has sent me to you.' This is My name forever, and this is how I am to be remembered in every generation.

[16] Go, assemble the elders of Israel and say to them, 'The LORD, the God of your fathers, the God of Abraham, Isaac, and Jacob, has appeared to me and said: I have surely attended to you and have seen what has been done to you in Egypt. [17] And I have promised to bring you up out of your affliction in Egypt, into the land of the Canaanites, Hittites, Amorites, Perizzites, Hivites, and Jebusites—a land flowing with milk and honey.'

[18] The elders of Israel will listen to what you say, and you must go with them to the king of Egypt and tell him, 'The LORD, the God of the Hebrews, has met with us. Now please let us take a three-day journey into the wilderness, so that we may sacrifice to the LORD our God.'

[19]But I know that the king of Egypt will not allow you to go unless a mighty hand compels him. [20] So I will stretch out

My hand and strike the Egyptians with all the wonders I will perform among them. And after that, he will release you. [21]And I will grant this people such favor in the sight of the Egyptians that when you leave, you will not go away empty-handed. [22] Every woman shall ask her neighbor and any woman staying in her house for silver and gold jewelry and clothing, and you will put them on your sons and daughters. So you will plunder the Egyptians."

[**3:1**] Notice that there was an ANGEL standing there. An angel. It stood near the bush, yes, but the angel was burning, not the bush. The bush did NOT burn, despite the presence of the angel. It was a burning angel next to a non-burning bush. In other words, it was not a regular fire.

[**3:8**] Again, the plan. It wasn't just about freedom. God had a purpose. He needed them to take back Canaan from the bad guys. The purpose was to purge Canaan, which everybody (Hebrews, Egyptians, and Canaanites) were surprised when Moses did not lead them directly into battle in CANAAN.

What's in a Name?

[**3:14**] The name. In Egyptian culture, there were five aspects of "being" that defined a human. The Akh, Ba, Ka, name, and shadow were all part of your identity. The entire basis of "mummies" comes from this concept. When Team Thebes took over, they tried to kill Nefertiti twice by destroying her corpse, her statues, and chiseling out her name. Just like our Book of Life described in the Book of Revelation, the Egyptians believed your name needed to be written down in order to achieve immortality. Pharaohs would write their names upon the pyramids

(1st block at the bottom :) to make sure their NAME would continue to exist. So when Moses asked GOD for his name, there was a cultural reason for this.

Yet God seems to sense this and responds coyly with "I am." Was God serious? Because Moses quickly scribbled down "I am," which became known as the Holy Name. Yet then God expands his identity by including the "God of…" titles.

Shortly after this (within a year or so), God gives Moses and the Hebrews the 10 Commandments. With it, he drops commandment #2:

[Exodus 20:7] Thou shalt not take the name of the LORD thy God in vain; for the LORD will not hold him guiltless that taketh his name in vain.

To me, this is more than just cussing. The ancient Egyptians saw magic and power in names, and if they remained steadfast in this belief, they'd be wanting to use it for spells and such, like they did in Egypt.

So was "I AM" an actual proper name?

The Hebrews seemed to believe so, which is why they developed the concept of the Tetragrammaton, which is a law where Jews are forbidden from using or writing the Holy Name Moses asked about. To avoid writing the word, the Hebrews wrote it with only consonants YHWH (Y vs. J debate ignored for now). As an English speaker/reader, I see the Holy Name written down as LORD throughout the Bible. The Hebrews would also avoid speaking it aloud, and when they got to it in text, they verbalized "Adonai" to keep the name holy. If you put YHWH and Andonai together, you'd have the full word.

But don't say it!

God is either a big jokester and gave Moses a "fake" name, which Moses wrote down to revere later, OR he gave him the legit name I AM, with a warning and commandment about its use.

How can we tell?

Well, Moses wrote the Pentateuch, and had bunches of opportunity to set the record straight. So what did he use?

Oh dear, he used all sorts of names.

From the plural Elohim to I AM, God has dozens of names and titles that Moses and other prophets use in the Old and New Testament. Moses certainly mixed up his use of names, which in turn, mixed me up a bit, too.

Because of the lack of clarity, early translators chose to respect the Hebrew tradition by not translating YHWH into an English word. Only in recent years have Christians insisted on using YHWH as a proper word, giving me a bit of anxiety. Better to err on the side of caution?

Genesis 4:26 also gives me pause. Why do we get a big section on "bad guys" from the Cain line, and then finish it with the idea that at "that time" men began to "use the name of the Lord." Notice how Moses wrote LORD. Moses connected the secret I AM response with the preflood world. However, I'm not sure if this is a good or bad thing. The preflood world was evil and needed to be destroyed by a flood. Did they "misuse" the name, which is the reason for Commandment #2? Did the "misuse" of the name contribute to the state of the fallen world? Yes, you can spin this as "worship" but then you're saying that Adam and Eve didn't worship God prior to this moment.

My "pause" does not change my relationship with God, and if I'm wrong, Fear of the Lord is not a bad thing. Let's just say I'm right and Commandment #2 is about not misusing the specific I AM name. Whoa...how do you misuse it. Is there power and magic in it?

Remember, in **Revelation 3:12**, Jesus alludes to getting a "new name" and then in 19:18, he has a name written upon his robe and thigh. A new world. A new name.

Okay, back to the calling…

[3:17] Notice how God does not include any names like Anakim, Zamzummim, Emim, or Horites. God mentions the humans but not the "other" names. This is another reason why I think we're dealing with paranormal monsters rather than hill tribes.

[3:20] Spoiler! I love how God ruins the suspense and establishes his omniscient ways by forecasting how everything is going down.

[3:22] Plunder. Again, 40 years earlier, Moses could have created a civil war and stolen the throne for Team Delta, but that was not God's plan. Nor was it God's need. He needed the Hebrews to clean up Canaan, yet he rewards them with the wealth of Egypt.

Milk, Honey, and Gold...all bait for humans who would need encouragement in the battle that was about to take place.

CHAPTER SEVEN

BATTLING BELIAL

"My name is Ozymandias, King of Kings,
look on my works, ye Mighty, and despair."

Ramses the Great, known as Ozymandias in Greece, or Junior to Ramses I, inherited the throne of Egypt at the age of 16. While not as young as King Tut, he was still pretty young. Historians see it as the beginning of a new dynasty, Dynasty 19, for he really doesn't have any connections to the slugfest between Team Delta and Team Thebes. While he has a powerful lineage, he's also descended from the hired help. The last bit of royal blood died with King Tut, who hired Horemheb, who hired Ramses I, who sired Seti, who sired Ramses the Great.

He sits on a stolen throne.

I'd like to give the kid the benefit of the doubt. After all, he had nothing to do with killing babies, enslaving the Hebrews, poisoning kings, killing suitors, or trying to assassinate Moses. When God gives Moses the "all clear," it would be easy to believe the threat is over and the throne will be receptive to the Hebrew plight.

How can a sixteen-year-old be a monster?

Ramses the Great is the greatest warrior, builder, and strategist in Egyptian history, according to...um, Ramses? Yep, I complained in lesson one that many sources of Egyptian history all come from the same era. Ramses celebrates his father and daughter with building projects, celebrates his own amazing conquests, and celebrates all things Egyptian.

Celebrate!

Ramses inherited a dynasty that was already strengthening its grasp over all of Egypt. With Team Delta utterly destroyed, and Moses most likely dead, Team Thebes began to build their own cities in the delta, which would allow Ramses the Great to expand the Egyptian empire to its mightiest best.

But what if Ramses was an insecure liar?

Scientists have recently studied the DNA of Ramses' mummy and determined that his hair color would have been red. A ginger? As a descendant of the hired help, I think the fact that he doesn't look like a typical Egyptian might factor into his thoughts and actions. While it would be easy to cast aspersions upon his hair color (Mark of Cain! Ah!) I think it simply supports a potentially insecure prince.

His glorious defeat of the Hittites? Insecurity.

His birth name (Ramses=Ra is the One who bore him)? Insecurity.

His preferred name (Ozymandias=The Maat of Ra is powerful)? Insecurity.

His long life and long rule? Insecurity.

His desecration of Amarna? Hold on, they are still breaking statues?

Yep. Gingermandias keeps flogging a dead horse. Does it promote nativism amongst the dark haired Egyptians? The ghost of Nefertiti still haunts Egypt and Gingermandias. They won, but they won't let it go. This is why I like to see him as rampantly insecure.

God Hardened His Heart

I cannot get into a debate on fate and free will or the concept of predestination. My MSU English Degree just can't handle something Luther and Erasmus couldn't settle. Yet when we get to Lesson Eight and the 10 plagues, we see it stated again and again that not only was Gingermandias' heart hardened but that God caused it.

This reminds me of another line from the Bible.

[John 17:12] While I was with them in the world, I kept them in thy name: those that thou gavest me I have kept, and none of them is lost, but the son of perdition; that the scripture might be fulfilled.

Context: This is Jesus after the last supper. He's now back on the Mount of Olives, and prepares his disciples (minus Judas) for the dark days ahead. During this moment, Jesus reflects on his mission coming to an end, including the creation of a church, to be started by the eleven disciples sitting around him. As you can clearly see, Jesus singles out Judas, saying that he was never one of them because Judas was a "son of perdition."

That is predestination.

Earlier, Jesus shows this when he says:

[John 6:70] Jesus answered them, "Have not I chosen you twelve, and one of you is a devil?"

See, Jesus knew the plan. It turns out (whether known or unknown) that Judas was the son of perdition, who was not "lost" along the way. How is he not "lost"? He never belonged to Jesus in the first place. He was a son of perdition.

I believe Gingermandias is cut from a similar cloth as Judas.

Yes, Horemheb was quite a villain. Before that, Amenhotep III used birth control and murder to wipe out a generation of Hebrews. On paper, Gingermandias only has a **"hard heart,"** which seems to be a distant third place in the celebrity evil games. Yet there are a few dark, disturbing details that shine a light into a very dark place.

First, Gingermandias promotes the worship of Seth, who is a chaos god in the Egyptian pantheon. Seth also kills his own brother, Osiris, and brutally hacks up his body, which is hidden. Seth is a bad dude, and Gingermandias digs his style.

Second, Bint-Anath. She is the firstborn daughter of Gingermandias with his wife Isetnofret. The new palace in the Delta, Pi-Ramesses, has numerous dedications to her. Dad dedicated a town to her. What a swell guy.

Unfortunately, Anath is the name for a goddess known for her insatiable, bloodthirsty ways, cunning, bestiality, sorcery, incest, and connections to other goddess icons such as Kali, Semiramis, Athena, and Ishtar. Oh yeah, she is Canaanite.

Canaanite...isn't that the same as...?

Yep, Gingermandias is worshipping Hyksos gods.

Publically Egyptian (Seth) but privately Hyksos (Anath).

So far, all of this conjecture is mostly found in Egyptian history. For the truly dark stuff, we'll need to jump into the Bible.

Wizard Battle

Now, I skipped over some nice Moses-moments ranging from a strange circumcision scene, the family reunion, and the bricks-straw snafu. By this time, Gingermandias certainly knows who Moses is and what he wants, which sets up quite a moment.

> **[Exodus 7:10] And Moses and Aaron went in unto Pharaoh, and they did so as the LORD had commanded: and Aaron cast down his rod before Pharaoh, and before his servants, and it became a serpent. [11] Then Pharaoh also called the wise men and the sorcerers: now the magicians of Egypt, they also did in like manner with their enchantments. [12] For they cast down every man his rod, and they became serpents: but Aaron's rod swallowed up their rods. [13] And he hardened Pharaoh's heart, that he hearkened not unto them; as the LORD had said.**

Gingermandias was ready for the showdown. In fact, he called in his sorcerers and had no issue matching miracle for miracle. Aaron's staff turned into a large snake? No problem…boys! Yep, our staffs can do the same thing. If you want to keep this minimalist, and the sorcerers had hollow chambers in their staff and it was all a trick…then how did they know what Aaron was going to do? Isn't prophecy just as miraculous? They KNEW Team God was going to do the old staff-snake trick so they created a meticulous deception intended to fake out the crowd.

Um, no.

Aaron's miracle happened spontaneously. The sorcerers still matched it.

How?!?

Don't get distracted by God's snake gobbling up their snake. That is cool but not the point. What trick allows this to happen? There is nothing natural about this scene. Remember, if my theory is true, Gingermandias is a secret Hyksos acolyte, and the symbol for the Hyksos regime was Apophis, serpent of destruction. God could have chosen to turn the staff into a goat and had a goat battle, but he chose the symbol for the Hyksos religion. Nice touch, God.

But How?!?

How did the sorcerers do this?

Before we get to the "how," let's look at who these guys were. Moses, who knew these guys personally, did not bother to give them a name or to even give Gingermandias a name, because, you know, NAME POWER!!!! Yet the Hebrews knew them and remembered. A millennium later, Paul name-drops these guys when making a point about evil.

[2 Timothy 3:8}: Now as Jannes and Jambres withstood Moses, so do these also resist the truth: men of corrupt minds, reprobate concerning the faith.

Jannes and Jambres. Okay.

Paul uses Greek to describe that these guys were "men of corrupt minds," which didn't really lead me anywhere. However, when I did a deeper search for Jannes and Jambres, I ran right into some interesting answers for "how" this happened.

So I went down another rabbit hole to find out if I could learn more about the men Paul mentioned in his letter to Timothy. Sure enough, there was A LOT of lore about them. Old-school Christian scholar Origen believed Paul was quoting an apocryphal book called *The Book of Jamnes and Jambres,* which is an apocryphal legend of their exploits. There are both Greek and Ethiopic (yes, more Tharbis) fragments, which were more likely than not known to the Qumran community (Dead Sea scrolls). While there are some name variations, the sorcerers are also described in *The Testament of Solomon*, Pliny the Elder's *Natural History,* the Gospel of Nicodemus, The Targum, Peor, Aggadic lore, The Book of Jasher, and the Zadokite fragments.

I'll save you some reading. They were *baaaad* dudes. Here is a segment that intrigued me from the Zadokite **"Belial will be let loose against Israel"** for it was Belial who inspired Jannes and Jambres to oppose Moses. Later it describes the **"three nets of Belial"** as fornication, wealth, and pollution of the sanctuary.

Paul said they were **"men of corrupt minds."** Was it because of Belial?

Belial=Perdition=Darkness=Death=Thanatos

There is a famous quotation out there from Charles Baudelaire that says, "The greatest trick the devil ever played was convincing the world he didn't exist."

I beg to differ.

If anything, the Devil is a *prima donna* that loves the spotlight and feeds his ego with claims that everything bad is his fault. He probably loves being seen as the great puppet master going toe to toe with God. It helps him forget that he was created to be a messenger (angel=malak=messenger) and a tutor for Adam and Eve in the Garden (Ez. 28). Even though it might have been another "predestination" moment, the Devil was once a good guy who fell.

It is Belial who has avoided the spotlight. Belial has made the world forget he (it) exists. Paul knew all about him.

I use an online Bible application that shows the top thirty English translations and compares them word to word. As an English teacher, I get how English can be a little tricky. Now, I like the old King James translation just to get insight into the world four centuries ago since publishing Bibles has become commercial and a new translation results in another opportunity to make money. Here is the old English version:

[2 Corinthians 6:14] Be ye not unequally yoked together with unbelievers: for what fellowship hath righteousness with unrighteousness? and what communion hath light with darkness? [15] And what concord hath Christ with Belial? or what part hath he that believeth with an infidel?

Before I get into the use of the word "belial," let's look at the nice juxtaposition made by Paul (the guy can write!). Paul sets up a series of comparisons so the folks of Corinth can more easily understand his point. He talks about their personal daily struggle and then compares it in the biggest, grandest struggle

Good	vs.	Evil
Corinthians	vs.	Unbelievers
Righteousness	vs.	Unrighteousness
Light	vs.	Darkness
Christ	vs.	Belial
Believeth (believer) vs.		Infidel (unbeliever)

Why did Paul bring up Belial? He could have made his point with good=light and evil=darkness, right? Instead, he brings up Christ, and since he is making comparisons, he needed to finish the comparison. What is the opposite of Christ? Beliar!

Paul wrote the Greek word Beliar in this verse, and of the 30 English translations, there were about five that translated it to "devil" or "Satan" while the other 80% of translations went with Belial (the English version of Beliar). Like with Nephilim, most gave us a new English word rather than a poor translation. I'm with the 80% here for a good reason. In the same letter to Corinth, Paul mentions Satan in verse 2:11. What did he write? Satana (Satan). If Beliar=Satan, then why didn't he use the same word?

Those five modern translations might want to white wash ALL EVIL under the umbrella of Satan, but Paul had a finer point to make. I have a finer point to make also.

Belial is the Darkness.

Let's go to St. John for a moment.

[John 1:1] In the beginning was the Word, and the Word was with God, and the Word was God. [2] The same was in the beginning with God. [3] All things were made by him; and without him was not any thing made that was made. [4] In him was life; and the life was the light of men. [5] And the light shineth in darkness; and the darkness comprehended it not.

Jesus=the Word=God=Light=Life

Darkness=

Ooh, big concepts here. If Jesus is life, then his true enemy is Death. Jesus existed as God the Creator, but when Adam and

Eve sinned, things went out of balance, and Jesus the Creator entered into the creation (weird concept for us) to fix it (Death).

This has little to do with Satan.

Want proof? Let's first ask Paul for his understanding.

[1 Corinthians 15:24] Then cometh the end, when he shall have delivered up the kingdom to God, even the Father; when he shall have put down all rule and all authority and power. [25] For he must reign, till he hath put all enemies under his feet. [26] The last enemy that shall be destroyed is death.

Okay, that wasn't super-obvious. Jesus will defeat enemies. Enemies? Destroyed? That is some heavy personification used there. During "the end," the last enemy to be destroyed is (D)eath? Still not clear on Belial, is it? Well, let's do a quick summary of the events in the Book of Revelation. There is plenty of "destroying" and there are lots of enemies mentioned.

Enemy	Destroyed	How
Babylon	Rev. 14:8	Catastrophe
The Antichrist	Rev. 19:20	Thrown in Lake of Fire
The Prophet	Rev. 19:20	Thrown in Lake of Fire
Gog and Magog	Rev. 20:9	Fire from Heaven
Satan	Rev. 20:10	Thrown in Lake of Fire
Hades	Rev. 20:14	Thrown in Lake of Fire
Death	Rev. 20:14	Thrown in Lake of Fire

Satan is not the penultimate enemy because it does not end with him. Paul previewed it. John prophesied it. The last enemy to be destroyed is Death. Death will be thrown, just like a man or dragon, into the Lake of Fire. It was Belial in the opening of John that could not comprehend the light of Jesus. Belial will be the last enemy in the Book of Revelation to be thrown into the Lake of Fire.

If Belial isn't on your radar, don't feel bad, but he's been hidden right in front of you in the Old Testament.

Belial Name Drop	Context
Judges 19:22	"Sons of Belial" gang rape
Deut 13:13	"Children of Belial" Abominations and Apostates
1 Sam 2:12	"Sons of Belial" wicked sons, did not know God
1 Sam 25:17	"Son of Belial" a curse/taunt
2 Sam 20:1	"A Man of Belial" A rebellious Benjamite.

Many translations have dropped the word Belial in favor of words like rebel, scoundrel, or pervert. In fact, the name Belial has a bunch of fascinating (and disturbing) name implications, with just a different emphasis on a different syllable. It's like the name of God except written in the Black Speech of Mordor (Lord of the Rings reference).

Belial directly translates as "May have no rising," which works if we're talking about the darkness, death, or the abyss.

Beli yo'il translates as "worthless."

Beli ol translates as "yokeless" which is a free will, rebel meaning.

Beli Ya'al translates as "never to rise," which also fits the abyss.

Bel Ya'al translates as "Lord of the Goats," which fits the inverted star pentagram as well as the Leviticus 16:8 scapegoat called Azazel (we'll talk about him later).

Baal ial translates as "Lord of Pride," which fits both Satan and/or his master.

These six slight variations show the complexity of this "evil one" as well as the difficulty for the English translators to take an old school Hebrew word and update it to English, yet the translators all knew the lore behind the word when they translated the old Hebrew word. There is a good reason for the context even in the last four centuries.

Belial Beyond

I'm about to throw out a lot of books and sources, knowing that many of them lack credibility. My point is that Belial was a known commodity for thousands of years and has only vanished from Christian awareness in recent centuries. For example, John Milton's ***Paradise Lost*** clearly featured Belial, not as a fallen angel, but as something else.

The reason?

Angels were created early in creation. Adam and Eve sinned after creation was complete. Their sin brought...DEATH. Yes, Milton had Belial coming last because Belial was Death incarnate. Yet today few even know the name Belial. Does this sound like a conspiracy theory? Or does it sound like a prophesied "falling away" near the End Times. Know Jesus, yes! Know thy enemy? Um...maybe?

The Book of Jubilees Describes the "uncircumcised heathen" as the Sons of Belial. So this one isn't very damning but it does help give a bit of negative connotation.

The Goetia In this spurious book credited to the original exorcist, Solomon (read Luke 11:14-32), Belial is described as the

King of Demons, made after Lucifer (aka Satan). This occult work is the guidebook to medieval magic and demons.

The War of the Sons of Light... This old text found with the Dead Sea Scrolls is a pretty epic tale of good and evil. The Sons of Light are the good guys and the Sons of Darkness are the bad guys. In this account, Belial is the leader of the Sons of Darkness. "But for corruption, thou has made Belial, an angel of hostility. All his dominions are in darkness, and his purpose is to bring wickedness and guilt. All the spirits that are associated with him are but angels of destruction."

The Testament of the Twelve Patriarchs is an old apocryphal collection that is pseudepigraphical (the author didn't really write them) accounts of the twelve sons of Jacob. Some consider a complete forgery, but for my purposes, it still shows what folks used to think about Belial. When written, it seemed to establish Belial in a dualist view as the enemy of God, which I reject for elevating Belial too high. Here are four excerpts:

Simeon 5:3 "fornication brings men close to Belial"

Levi 19:1 choose between "works of God" vs. "works of Belial." A disturbed soul is ruled over by Belial.

Naphtali Men must choose between God and Belial

Joseph Egypt was in darkness with Belial after Exodus. When the Messiah comes, the angels will bind Belial and give his children the power to trample spirits. Check.

The Ascension of Isaiah is another pseudepigraphical/apocryphal Christian-Jewish text that is pretty old but not trustworthy. Again, it gives insight into Belial. In the text, it describes Belial as the angel of lawlessness who is "the ruler of this world." I guess that is why Satan is only considered the "Prince" of darkness, even in the Bible. Belial is King (of the fallen world)? Belial also has a special name, is accursed by God, and is known as "the Angel of Darkness." There are some strange, deep philosophies, including God's claim "I shall not retrain Belial within my heart," which is strange when comparing God saying about Adam and Eve, they have become like "Us, knowing Good and Evil." Huh? Deep thoughts! It finishes by describing that the mystery of God is that we cannot understand why God allows Belial to exist. The last enemy indeed!

The Satanic Bible I know! I know! I know! Whether you view these folks as lunatics or true enemies, they know God/Jesus as their enemy yet celebrate evil. Sure enough, they also know Belial as one of the four crown princes of hell, the earth element, and the representation of the carnal.

New Advent (Catholic Encyclopedia): To cleanse your spiritual palate, I'll finish with the Catholic view of Belial (which may or may not help). "He is the prince of this world and will come as Antichrist," found as a personal name in the Vulgate, "the personification of evil." The Antichrist? Where did that come from?

Well, it connects to the idea of being a "son of Perdition." Judas is labeled as a "son of Perdition," and then Paul describes (2 Thes 2:3) a "man of sin" in the End Times with the same phrase, "the son of Perdition." In the Book of Revelation, there is a slight reference found in Rev 17:8 with **"the beast that goes into Perdition."** If you add on:

> **[1 John 2:18] Little children, it is the last time: and as ye have heard that antichrist shall come, even now are there many antichrists; whereby we know that it is the last time.**

John expands the definition of the antichrist, which seems to fit the "son of Perdition" concept instead of an ultimate villain. Now, compare that to the "perdition" reference in Rev 17, and you might see why John expands the definition:

[Rev 17:9] And here is the mind which hath wisdom. The seven heads are seven mountains, on which the woman sitteth. [10] And there are seven kings: five are fallen, and one is, and the other is not yet come; and when he cometh, he must continue a short space. [11] And the beast that was, and is not, even he is the eighth, and is of the seven, and goeth into perdition."

That was a total of eight "sons of perdition" or "antichrists" that John referenced.

The Catholic perspective is that Belial will have a connection to the Antichrist, and the word Perdition means "apoleian" in Greek. Sound familiar? Revelation 9:11 has a personalized Greek name Apollyon, which means "the Destroying One" (In Hebrew, it is Abaddon). As an English teacher, I would call one a common noun and the other a proper noun. Remember, Apollyon is locked up in an Abyss, and the name Belial literally means the opposite of "rise."

Many cultures like the Greeks believed a soul would descend to the underworld, where the Olympian Hades rules. But even to the Greeks, Thanatos was the far more powerful God of Death. Hades was more of a "gatekeeper" figure. During the time of Christ, the Greek word thanatos was used in all sorts of ways (120 occurrences) to describe the concept of death, so it is difficult to determine when the Proper Noun or the common noun was intended.

So when I heard that Ramses the Great, Ozymandias, or Gingermandias as I like to tease, had priests affiliated with Belial, I knew I was dealing with a PRIME VILLAIN, perhaps even one of the "seven heads" that John wrote about in Rev 17. Even Nebuchadnezzar acknowledged God and fell to his knees. Gingermandias? Nothing! His heart is hard. Also, don't forget that he directly worships Seth and named his daughter after Anath.

As much as I'd like to get back to Moses, I'd like to first finish my points with Belial.

The Other Guy

Earlier, I made an argument that Belial = Perdition = Darkness = Death = Thanatos. Well, Revelation 20 mentions two enemies with Proper noun names:

[Revelation 20] And the sea gave up the dead which were in it; and death and hell delivered up the dead which were in them: and they were judged every man according to their works.

The old King James Version was the beginning of the end for Proper Names. In Greek, it read "Thanatos and Hades." Now, I've already explained that I believe Belial is the Hebrew word for Thanatos, so who is the Hebrew equivalent for Hades?

First, I find it interesting that Thanatos and Hades are paired together in other spots of the Bible also. Believing Thanatos = Apollyon = Abaddon, I also looked for Abaddon references in the Old Testament.

Revelation 1:18	The keys of Death (Thanatos) and Hades
Revelation 6:8	Death (Thanatos) rides/ Hades follows
Job 26:6	Sheol is naked, Abaddon has no covering
Job 28:22	Abaddon and Death say...

Job 31:12	It is a fire that burns down to Abaddon
Psalm 88:11	Being in Abaddon
Proverb 15:11	Sheol and Abaddon lie open...

Remember, in the Old Testament, Hebrew was used, so the word Hades will not appear organically in the original texts. Hell follows the same rule and was only used by English speakers who were once conquered by Vikings (Hela=goddess of death/Helheim=place of death) in the A.D. era. So the Jews had a place (sheol=hades) as well as a Proper Noun (Sheol=Hades) for the other bad guy.

The last two enemies (still not Satan).

Did Jesus ever distinguish the two?

Well, Jesus used the word "Gehenna" as a reference to the "burning place," which in His divine mind was probably thinking the "Lake of Fire." But in another spot, like Paul, he clearly distinguishes two villains.

> **[Luke 11:14] And he was casting out a devil, and it was dumb. And it came to pass, when the devil was gone out, the dumb spake; and the people wondered. [15] But some of them said, He casteth out devils through <u>Beelzebub the chief of the devils.</u> [16] And others, tempting him, sought of him a sign from heaven. [17] But he, knowing their thoughts, said unto them, Every kingdom divided against itself is brought to desolation; and a house divided against a house falleth. [18] <u>If Satan</u> also be divided against himself, how shall his kingdom stand? because ye say that I cast out devils through Beelzebub. [19] And if I by Beelzebub cast out devils, by whom do your sons cast them out? therefore shall they be your judges. [20] But if I with the finger of God cast out devils, no doubt the kingdom of God is come upon you.**

First, the backstory. Jesus was exorcising demons, which was normally done by a team of Jewish exorcists who used an exorcism book dating back to Solomon (not sure if that is from Solomon, but it is a real text). When Jesus just showed up and used his authority as the Son of God (instead of the textbook), this upset the exorcists. They cried foul, and since Jesus didn't use the book, they assumed he was in league with the demons. Clear now?

Second, Jesus's point: That's stupid! Yep, Jesus said they don't make any sense. If he were an agent of darkness, why would he work against his own team by fixing the poor possessed fellow? Then later, he goes and mocks the "Solomon" exorcists by saying:

> **[Luke 11:31] The queen of the south shall rise up in the judgment with the men of this generation, and condemn them: for she came from the utmost parts of the earth to hear the wisdom of Solomon; and, behold, a greater than Solomon is here."**

Finally, my point. Jesus knows how Heaven and Earth work. In his rebuke of the exorcists, he brings up TWO figures. First, he establishes "Team Darkness" as anything having to do with demons. Next, he mentions (Satanas) as part of "Team Darkness." Then, he acknowledges that he is breaking the rules by referencing not only the exorcism rules but also the figure Beelzebub (Beezeboul). Jesus acknowledges that both figures are from "Team Darkness" and would not be working against each other in their war against God/Holy Spirit/Jesus. It's a good point.

So who is this Beelzebub figure (rolling up my sleeves)?

THE LORD OF THE FLIES!

Okay, I'm an English teacher, so I got really excited for one of my favorite books. Let me first explain the lore behind Beelzebub. From the Solomon exorcists to Shakespeare, Beelzebub was known as the "gatekeeper" of the underworld. Some folks will say Beelzebub is a nickname for Satan, but then why would Jesus differentiate the name? Jesus used two names for two Proper Nouns to make his point about a "house divided."

Like Charon the Ferryman from Greek mythology, Beelzebub opened and closed the Gates of Sheol (Underworld, Hades, Hell). Didn't know about the gates? Check out: Psalm 24:9, Psalm 107, Job 38:17, Isaiah 38:10, Isaiah 45:2, Matt 16:18. Even Jesus references the Gates of Hades. How's that for gates?

But how did Beelzebub become known as the Gatekeeper?

There is an old third century pseudepigraphal text called **The Gospel of Nicodemus**. Again, it is not canon for a reason, but it was still a real book that Christians read or referenced. Whether divine or not, it tells an interesting story of what happened during the three days Jesus was dead. Remember how the dead rose and walked around (Matt 27:52)? Well, the **Gospel of Nicodemus** tells the tale of two recently dead sons of Simeon, Charinus and Lenthius, and what they saw while in the Underworld.

They tell Joseph of Arimathea how they met the righteous dead, such as Adam, Isaiah, and even Seth (from Genesis). In the tale, Satan and Beelzebub get in a fight. Beelzebub is upset that someone took one of his dead (Lazarus). When this happens, David and Isaiah (despite being dead) get very excited and explain to the Sons of Simeon how their prophecies predicted the coming of Christ to bust them out of the Underworld.

Sure enough, a few weeks pass, and Satan is celebrating the death of Jesus. Beelzebub is both angry and fearful. He knows Jesus died without sin, and thus, has no part of being dead. This cosmic law causes his gates to break open, allowing Jesus the opportunity to steal the righteous dead (from Abraham's Bosom, the good side of Sheol, Paradise). Beelzebub and Satan practically fist fight, and Jesus "gives Satan" and authority to Beelzebub as some sort of prize (Still a bad guy though). Jesus brings the dead to Michael so he can get topside to continue the Easter scene at the tomb with Mary Magdalene.

So that is why both Jews and early Christians knew the name Beelzebub.

The origin of the word, though, goes all the way back to the days of Moses (which will finally let me bring this chapter to a close).

Shortly after Moses dies, Joshua and the Hebrews prepare for a long war for possession of Canaan. Knowing this, the Canaanites prepare for the arrival of the Hebrews from the wilderness. According to the legend, all along the western border, the vile Canaanites left warnings for the invaders to not "mess with us." To show their resolve, the Canaanites went out into the edges of the wilderness to build stone altars (not so scary).

Upon these altars, they made sacrifices (okay, a little gross).

When the advance scouts from the Hebrew army arrived at the altars, large swarms of flies would rise up like clouds. Why? They were feasting on the rotting flesh (really gross).

What kind of flesh? Not animal. Not even sacrificed prisoners of war (that would have been scary). Nope, the vile Canaanites took their own children and sacrificed them upon these altars. So when the advance scouts saw the pile of little kids and gasped, puked, fainted, or cursed, they quickly understood the resolve of the people they were facing.

It was the calling card for the Lord of the Flies.

In Hebrew, Baal=Lord (Not to be confused with YWHW) and Zebub/Zeboul means either Lord of the House or Lord of the Flies. Pretty clear in this case.

Yes, it would be simple and easy to just call it "Satanic" but the Old Testament clearly uses the Proper Names for two villains...Satan and Baal.

Baal was the Canaanite storm god and the incestuous lover of Anath, who Ramses the Great, Gingermandias, worshipped by naming his firstborn daughter after. They left Egypt and a single Baal worshipper for an entire nation of Baal worshippers. Gulp!

So when Gingermandias goes out of his way to eradicate worship of Aten, it is an act of evil. When he promotes the worship of Seth, it is evil. When he names his daughter after Anath, it is evil. When he surrounds himself with sorcerers of Belial, it is evil.

God is not just going to free the slaves; He is also going teach evil a lesson.

Cue the plagues...

CHAPTER EIGHT

PLAGUING THE GODS

Was the conflict ever in doubt?

Really?

Is it an even match for the Master of the Universe, the Lord God Almighty, capital G.O.D. to take on a pampered Egyptian brat? Well, God knew the outcome before he even sent Moses, including the fact that Ramses the Great's heart would remain unchanged. It is my theory that this was not about humbling a man but humbling the forces of evil. There is a war waged between the lines. At minimum, the Hebrews had spent four hundred years surrounded by false gods. This war will take those beliefs down a peg and put the God of Abraham up a few pegs. Seeing is believing, right? At most epic (and you know I love EPIC), God is putting a collection of fallen angels in their places. He begins with those in Egypt and will then move on to those in Canaan.

I'm sure some of you are struggling with my epic lens. There are no other gods but God. Well, let's look at what God actually said about the matter.

[Genesis 20:1] And God spake all these words, saying, [2] I am the LORD thy God, which have brought thee out of the land of Egypt, out of the house of bondage. [3] Thou shalt have no other gods before me. [4] Thou shalt not make unto thee any graven image, or any likeness of anything that is in heaven above, or that is in the earth beneath, or that is in the water under the earth: [5] Thou shalt not bow down thyself to them, nor serve them: for I the LORD thy God am a jealous God, visiting the iniquity of the fathers upon the children unto the third and fourth generation of them that hate me; [6] And showing mercy unto thousands of them that love me, and keep my commandments.

Now, if there was no such thing as the boogey man, why didn't God just say with the first commandment, "I am the only God. Everything else is make-believe?" Instead, God establishes the following inferences:

A. There are other gods (whatever that means)
B. Some are in/from "heaven" (whatever that means).
C. Some are in/from the earth (like Egypt/Canaan?).
D. Some are "under the earth" (whatever that means).
E. God is jealous (in a good way) of our loyalties.
F. Worshiping the "gods" will bring generations of ill will.

That is pretty intense for something that doesn't exist. Yes, you can "metaphor" this away. You can turn "a god" into a sin or addiction quite easily, but back in the days of Moses, we had elemental transformation (the staffs) and the Priests of Belial will go "miracle for miracle" on a few of the plagues. That was pretty literal. In the Book of Revelation, there seems to be some pretty literal enemies being thrown into a Lake of Fire, too. Why don't we see epic displays of magic and gods in 2020? Well, the context of Exodus alludes to God cleaning house of all the dirt left behind after the flood. I believe all the magic-making, giant-daddies will be taken off the board, leaving only Satan and some demon-spawn left by the time of Christ.

Look at how many are mentioned in the Bible: Amon, Asherah, Ashtoreth, Baal, Beelzebub, Bel, Chemosh, Dagon, Gad, Artemis, Jupiter (Zeus), Mercury (Hermes), Merodach, Milcom, Molech, Nebo, the Queen of Heaven, Tammuz…

There are thirty-four clear references to gods, whether real or not. Yes, the graven images and idols could have been a bunch of hogwash, but there is a lot of purpose in deconstructing the Egyptian gods by God. It seems he is doing more than just "re-cruiting through miracles" and is also "putting gods in their places."

The First Plague: Blood

First, let's preview the miracle about to happen. I'm not go-ing to argue any sort of reasonable cause for this because the text does not allow "reason" to explain erosion, pollution, or natural catastrophe. This passage defies the laws of physics (which God wrote, so...he can suspend at any time?).

Growing up, I've seen some pretty toxic water that will sup-port a yellow-bellied bullhead. I've seen spring flooding that turn rivers into muddy, foaming cesspools...but still the fish found a way. In Egypt, the water becomes toxic either because of unex-plained pollution upstream or...IT WAS REALLY BLOOD.

Watch how the water works. God turns it into blood in front of Pharaoh, not as an explainable flow from a source upstream. Even if you wanted the miracle to be: A. God causes pollution way upstream, B. tells Moses it is coming, C. Moses times it just right so the tainted water arrived just when Ramses is taking a morning wash, and D. Lasts exactly for seven days (A God number), that still requires God to manage it all…naturally. If your God can do all of that, why can't He control physics and elements also? The water does not obey this God-timed, natural plague. If it was flow, then why was the existing water that had been 'Mosesed' (just kidding. Dad joke. Moses means "drawn from water") err...drawn from the Nile previously (just start over). WHY WAS THAT WATER CHANGED?

Yep, the water in wooden and stone vessels was turned to blood also. Both the Egyptians and Hebrews are lazy. You don't want to go down to the Nile every time you need a drink, so send the kids down to the river, fill up the pitchers and buckets, and you can have water at your house for days at a time (prior to the invention of water towers). Yet this passage explains that on the day of the miracle, even the reserves were changed to blood.

This is a comprehensive miracle.

[Exodus 7:14] And the LORD said unto Moses, Pharaoh's heart is hardened, he refuseth to let the people go. [15] Get thee unto Pharaoh in the morning; lo, he goeth out unto the water; and thou shalt stand by the river's brink against he come; and the rod which was turned to a serpent shalt thou take in thine hand. [16] And thou shalt say unto him, The LORD God of the Hebrews hath sent me unto thee, saying, Let my people go, that they may serve me in the wilderness: and, behold, hitherto thou wouldest not hear. [17] Thus saith the LORD, In

this thou shalt know that I am the LORD: behold, I will smite with the rod that is in mine hand upon the waters which are in the river, and they shall be turned to blood. [18] And the fish that is in the river shall die, and the river shall stink; and the Egyptians shall loath to drink of the water of the river. [19] And the LORD spake unto Moses, Say unto Aaron, Take thy rod, and stretch out thine hand upon the waters of Egypt, upon their streams, upon their rivers, and upon their ponds, and upon all their pools of water, that they may become blood; and that there may be blood throughout all the land of Egypt, both in vessels of wood, and in vessels of stone. [20] And Moses and Aaron did so, as the LORD commanded; and he lifted up the rod, and smote the waters that were in the river, in the sight of Pharaoh, and in the sight of his servants; and all the waters that were in the river were turned to blood. [21] And the fish that was in the river died; and the river stank, and the Egyptians could not drink of the water of the river; and there was blood throughout all the land of Egypt. [22] And the magicians of Egypt did so with their enchantments: and Pharaoh's heart was hardened, neither did he hearken unto them; as the LORD had said. [23] And Pharaoh turned and went into his house, neither did he set his heart to this also. [24] And all the Egyptians dug round about the river for water to drink; for they could not drink of the water of the river. [25] And seven days were fulfilled, after that the LORD had smitten the river.

As an English teacher, I have to take a moment to discuss to cool symbolism first. Eighty years earlier, Pharaoh Amenhotep III attempted genocide, and he used the Nile as an accomplice to murder a generation of Hebrews. The crocodiles would have turned the Nile into a river of blood.

Now let's talk about a couple of strange passages. First, let's address Jannes and Jambres. These guys had gumption. All of the water drawn from the Nile River was turned to blood, which meant there was blood everywhere! Shocking stuff! Gingermandias not only believed these guys could do the same thing, but Jannes and Jambres actually had a plan. AND THEN THEY DID IT! If you don't want the passage to have multiple miracles, then you could wish for a Kool-Aid trick, but the omniscient POV narration written years later by Moses with (fire-pillar God/Jesus/Holy Spirit) dictating did not say "and the magicians through deceit tricked Pharaoh." It said they "did so."

So where did they get the clear water? Ah, that is curious. They dug wells. Living next to a river, you normally don't need a well, especially with the Nile being super-reliable. Why was the well water not tainted? It came from rain, which collected as groundwater before slowly seeping into the Nile. Only the Nile River water was affected.

God had a purpose in his narrow miracle.

The Target

The mythology teacher is going to come out now. Like our *Genesis*, the Egyptians believed the world started with water. They have a quartet of gods known as the Ogdoad, with Nun being the god of water, Amen being the god of invisibility, Heh being infinity, and Kek being darkness. With GOD snapping his fingers and turning Nun into blood, Moses showed Pharaoh who the master of the water truly was.

Another Egyptian god is Hapi (happy? Ironically, his symbol was the mushroom…dude!). Hapi is the god of the Nile, so GOD is really picking on him. Only "Hapi water" was turned to blood. Without any backstory, I have no idea the "fallen angel" being worshipped here, but God put this former servant into its place.

The Second Plague: Frogs

Frogs are kinda cute, so this is a curious curse. Easily killed with a step, the frogs would have started to pile up just by walking around. So why cute? Both with the 10 Plagues and the Book of Revelation, God is portrayed as being full of vengeance: The WRATH OF GOD! Folks often see the End Times as God destroying the earth because he's mean and mad. Part of his reason in giving us the specific details is because he loves us. He wants evil folks to repent. The signs in the Book of Revelation are "last chances" to change your ways. Each one that ticks off should be seen as another opportunity to get right with God. This is not cruel. It is an opportunity.

Here, we have frogs, who don't harm anyone. It annoys, but does not impact. Heck, it's a good food source with a lack of quality fish around. No fish mean all the tadpoles grew up? I'm not going to even tackle the "natural miracle" of this.

I do want you to notice that Jannes and Jambres AGAIN shrug their shoulders and turn to Belial for another miracle, which is granted. Say what? How did they produce frogs? It doesn't explain.

> **[Exodus 8:1] And the LORD spake unto Moses, Go unto Pharaoh, and say unto him, Thus saith the LORD, Let my people go, that they may serve me. [2] And if thou refuse to let them go, behold, I will smite all thy borders with frogs: [3] And the river shall bring forth frogs abundantly, which shall go up**

and come into thine house, and into thy bedchamber, and upon thy bed, and into the house of thy servants, and upon thy people, and into thine ovens, and into thy kneading troughs: [4] And the frogs shall come up both on thee, and upon thy people, and upon all thy servants. [5] And the LORD spake unto Moses, Say unto Aaron, Stretch forth thine hand with thy rod over the streams, over the rivers, and over the ponds, and cause frogs to come up upon the land of Egypt. [6]And Aaron stretched out his hand over the waters of Egypt; and the frogs came up, and covered the land of Egypt. [7] And the magicians did so with their enchantments, and brought up frogs upon the land of Egypt. [8] Then Pharaoh called for Moses and Aaron, and said, Entreat the LORD, that he may take away the frogs from me, and from my people; and I will let the people go, that they may do sacrifice unto the LORD. [9] And Moses said unto Pharaoh, Glory over me: when shall I entreat for thee, and for thy servants, and for thy people, to destroy the frogs from thee and thy houses, that they may remain in the river only? [10] And he said, To morrow. And he said, Be it according to thy word: that thou mayest know that there is none like unto the LORD our God. [11] And the frogs shall depart from thee, and from thy houses, and from thy servants, and from thy people; they shall remain in the river only. [12] And Moses and Aaron went out from Pharaoh: and Moses cried unto the LORD because of the frogs which he had brought against Pharaoh. [13] And the LORD did according to the word of Moses; and the frogs died out of the houses, out of the villages, and out of the fields. [14] And they gathered them together upon heaps: and the land stank. [15] But when Pharaoh saw that there was respite, he hardened his heart, and hearkened not unto them; as the LORD had said.

The Target

A frog god? Yep. In the beginning God hovered over the face of the waters. Well, the Egyptians saw Nun as the equivalent as Elohim (God) in the creation story. As a result, they saw watery Nun as a life-giver, and the symbol of Nun was the frog. Moses/God calling forth a swarm of frogs caused the Egyptians to curse their life-giving god.

Several chapters ago, I mentioned Hatshepsut as a "princess mother" candidate for the Moses timeline. According to Egyptologists, Hatshepsut worshipped another frog god called Heqet. Heqet was a goddess of childbirth, so I can see why folks choose her as the princess, but when you look a little closer at Heqet, it quickly gets darker. Yes, Heqet was a powerful female goddess who you'd pray to for help in getting pregnant, but her worship was a bit more sinister and had some surprising connotations. Ever read MacBeth? Well, Lady MacBeth was blood-smearing psychopath who'd do anything to become queen. What made her so mean and ruthless? Apparently, like Hatshepsut, she had problems with fertility and could not give MacBeth an heir. Who did she worship? Hecate. Now, Shakespeare knew his mythology also and took the Greek variation of the goddess Heqet, who was very pro-woman (Double, Double, toil and trouble) but was also vicious (something wicked this way comes). Hecate/Heqet was a goddess of witchcraft and sorcery who would stand at the crossroads at night with her hellhounds and lure wary travelers with her torch, and when the traveler got near, one of her three heads would turn and she'd club them to death with a mallet. 3 witches...3 heads...past, present, future. A true trinity of evil. Lady Macbeth and Hatshepsut turned to this evil frog goddess to give them children.

Remember the midwives who were told by Amenhotep III to kill the male Hebrew babies? Ah, Heqet was the goddess of childbirth, so...frog plague. God does hold grudges to the third and fourth generation.

Plague Three: Wee Bugs

Gnats or Lice? Both are small and annoying, so I guess it doesn't matter what word your translator picked because IT IS NOT NATURAL. It was not a byproduct of a food chain gone awry, but a Genesisish (nice adjective, huh?) miracle. Once again, life came from nothing. God creates life.

Jannes and Jambres? Well, as Priests of Belial, they can certainly manipulate chemistry/physics as well as command animals. Create life? Nope. Even something as small as gnats or lice could not be replicated. Wherever they got their previous magic (Belial), it does not have the authority to create life. Remember the Nephilim? They modified life (the giants) yet did not create anything from scratch. God just replicated the first week of creation.

Also notice how the Priests of Belial suddenly recognized the workmanship of God. Who did they think was giving Moses the power before this? See, they also believe in a pantheon of fallen gods until confronted by the authority of the Creator. It reminds me of the witch from Acts 16 and Balaam from Numbers 22-23; both used magic and both realized the true authority of God over their own powers.

[Exodus 8:16] And the LORD said unto Moses, Say unto Aaron, Stretch out thy rod, and smite the dust of the land, that it may become lice throughout all the land of Egypt. [17] And they did so; for Aaron stretched out his hand with his rod, and smote the dust of the earth, and it became lice in man, and in beast; all the dust of the land became lice throughout all the land of Egypt. [18] And the magicians did so with their enchantments to bring forth lice, but they could not: so there were lice upon man, and upon beast. [19] Then the magicians said unto Pharaoh, This is the finger of God: and Pharaoh's heart was hardened, and he hearkened not unto them; as the LORD had said.

The Target:

Another creator God of the Egyptians is Geb. Ready for some alliteration? Geb is the god of the ground and his symbol is the goose. So in the first three plagues, God has reminded all the Egyptians that neither Nun nor Geb had any true power and He was the true Creator.

Plague Four: Flies

Explain this…

So far, the miracles shown were either rationally explicable phenomenon or could be done through the mystical arts. When we get to the plague of flies, things begin to change. This time, the swarm of flies only affects the Egyptians as a sign that God is picking sides. Prior to this, frogs hopped in Hebrew houses, where the water had been turned to blood and the owner was itching because of little bugs. Now, the swarms of flies only affect the Egyptians.

The land of Goshen, where the former Team Delta lived as well as a majority of the brick-making slave population, received little to no effect. In central and southern Egypt, where Team Thebes lives, they are heavily plagued. Regardless of location, no Hebrew is bit.

[Exodus 8:20] And the LORD said unto Moses, Rise up early in the morning, and stand before Pharaoh; lo, he cometh forth to the water; and say unto him, Thus saith the LORD, Let my people go, that they may serve me. [21] Else, if thou wilt not let my people go, behold, I will send swarms of flies upon thee, and upon thy servants, and upon thy people, and into thy houses: and the houses of the Egyptians shall be full of swarms of flies, and also the ground whereon they are. [22] And I will sever in that day the land of Goshen, in which my people dwell, that no swarms of flies shall be there; to the end thou mayest know that I am the LORD in the midst of the earth. [23] And I will put a division between my people and thy people: to morrow shall this sign be. [24] And the LORD did so; and there came a grievous swarm of flies into the house of Pharaoh, and into his servants' houses, and into all the land of Egypt: the land was corrupted by reason of the swarm of flies.

The Target:

Khepri is not an Egyptian god I knew well from my mythology class, but he is a creator god whose scarab beetle form symbolizes birth and rebirth.

So not too much for symbolism.

However, if Gingermandias is indeed a "son of perdition," and he really worships the Hyksos/Canaanite gods, then this might have more meaning. Remember, Prince Baal is their favorite deity, even if Gingermandias worships Anath, and forty years from this moment, when the Hebrews and Joshua are crossing into the promised land, they will change the name Baal into Baalzebub, or Lord of the Flies. Perhaps the evil Canaanite trick of child sacrifice has already been in practice, explaining the anachronistic use of flies for Baal.

Plague Five: Livestock (err...deadstock?)

It has been a tough year for Nile River farmers. Bloody water, bugs, and frogs certainly made it tough to deal with your sheep, cows, and camels. It also makes me wonder how much time passes between these miracles? It really doesn't clarify, although my assumption has always been back-to-back-to-back....

This time, the specificity of the plagues shows that it isn't just a racial issue. I can just picture a racist Egyptian saying that Hebrews are unworthy of fly bites. This plague, however, supernaturally distinguishes one cow from another.

Having grown up on a farm in the 80s, I saw ear tags to identify ownership, etc. Did the ancient farmers have a similar system? Must've known somehow.

[Exodus 9:1] Then the LORD said unto Moses, Go in unto Pharaoh, and tell him, Thus saith the LORD God of the Hebrews, Let my people go, that they may serve me. [2] For if thou refuse to let them go, and wilt hold them still, [3] Behold, the hand of the LORD is upon thy cattle which is in the field, upon the horses, upon the asses, upon the camels, upon the oxen, and upon the sheep: there shall be a very grievous murrain. [4] And the LORD shall sever between the cattle of Israel and the cattle of Egypt: and there shall nothing die of all that is the children's of Israel. [5] And the LORD appointed a set time, saying, To morrow the LORD shall do this thing in the land. [6] And the LORD did that thing on the morrow, and

all the cattle of Egypt died: but of the cattle of the children of Israel died not one. [7] And Pharaoh sent, and, behold, there was not one of the cattle of the Israelites dead. And the heart of Pharaoh was hardened, and he did not let the people go.

The Target:

Hathor is the cow goddess of creation (how many creator gods did they have?). If there was such a thing as a redneck Egyptian, this plague hit home. I remember one of my students "recreating" Hathor the cow giving birth to the universe, which was quite a sight when other students began to drop out of the cardboard cow onto the floor like newborn gods. The myth of Hathor involves humans failing to worship the gods, and as punishment, Hathor went down to earth as a bloodthirsty killing plague. One problem...once she started killing humans, she could not stop, and if she killed all the humans, there would be no one left to worship them. So the other Egyptian gods got crafty, and voila! Beer was invented. It was dark beer, so it confused bloodthirsty Hathor, who drank it down, got drunk, and passed out, ending the bloodbath.

So not only did Hathor symbolize creation to local farmers, but she also represented beer. Shots fired, indeed.

Plague Six: Boils

Again, I like the parallel between the plagues and the Book of Revelation. After only impacting nature, God now turns up the dial on the nonbelievers, specifically the Priests of Belial, Jannes and Jambres. In Revelation, it reminds me of the Fifth Trumpet, where men are so tormented they seek death but cannot find it. The source of the Egyptian plague can only be attributed to Moses, who took the dormant ashes from a furnace and caused the disease to spread.

> **[Exodus 9:8] And the LORD said unto Moses and unto Aaron, Take to you handfuls of ashes of the furnace, and let Moses sprinkle it toward the heaven in the sight of Pharaoh. [9] And it shall become small dust in all the land of Egypt, and shall be a boil breaking forth with blains upon man, and upon beast, throughout all the land of Egypt. [10] And they took ashes of the furnace, and stood before Pharaoh; and Moses sprinkled it up toward heaven; and it became a boil breaking forth with blains upon man, and upon beast. [11] And the magicians could not stand before Moses because of the boils; for the boil was upon the magicians, and upon all the Egyptians. [12] And the LORD hardened the heart of Pharaoh, and he hearkened not unto them; as the LORD had spoken unto Moses.**

The Target:

The goddess of medicine was Isis (not the Islamic State in Syria). Isis was a strong female deity who was the consort of Osiris and mother of Hathor. Her symbol was the mother hen (like in Psalm 91), who would vigorously defend her chicks. When her husband was murdered by Seth (the guy Gingermandias worships), she goes on an epic quest for revenge and justice. Many scoffers reference Isis holding the wrapped body of slain Osiris as the origin of the idea for Mary holding Jesus at the foot of the cross. Nowhere in the Gospels does it say Mary scooped up Jesus when taken from the cross, but even if it did, a modern artist can still use the visual from another art form (Egyptian) without it meaning Christianity was a fabrication. Isis is also a figure that spans dynasty after dynasty. Every Egyptian knew Isis, who had healing arts.

There is another target besides Isis.

Remember how I got all excited about the "sons of perdition" talk? St. John not only went on record by saying there were "many antichrists" that had already come, but in the Book of Revelation, he talked about the seven heads of the beast being seven kings, and that five of them had already come (so...dead), one of them was/is (so...alive in the 1st century), and one of them would come (so...the future). These seven kings would somehow make an eighth...the nastiest of all nasty antichrists. In other words, the sons of perdition.

So I obsessed over the notion of trying to figure out who the previous "antichrists" were. For all the various reasons in this book, Gingermandias is one of them. In charting all the named villains in the Old Testament, I also found out that Nimrod had tons of evil lore. Josephus wrote that Nimrod built the Tower of Babel to not only survive another flood but to attack God. Nimrod was a bad dude. In my Nimrod-era research, I came across an interesting theory that Nimrod the Builder was the same figure as Imhotep the Builder. In Egyptian lore, Imhotep was a human who achieved godlike status. He was most famous for being a builder, but he is also famous for being the inventor of medicine. His timeline was also a thousand years prior to Moses, so that kinda lines up with Nimrod. First mention of Imhotep? That would be Amenhotep III (baby-killer Pharaoh), so that kinda works too.

If Nimrod=Imhotep holds up, then this plague has a very specific purpose in slamming the previous "Son of Perdition" from the days of Abraham. Ironically, in the Jewish tales of

Abraham vs. Nimrod, it was a swarm of gnats that defeated Nimrod's army.

Plague Seven: Hail

Today, Egypt is characterized for its sandy deserts in contrast with the lush Nile valley. This next plague makes me wonder how long it has been like that. Earlier, Moses negotiated terms of worship, which meant going three days into the wilderness. Now, I imagine the request was made in Thebes, which meant those Hebrews (especially his family) around Thebes would have joined Moses in a three-day walk into the desert to worship away from the angry eyes of the Egyptians.

A typical human can walk 3 mph, and since it is flat and sandy beyond the Nile, this seems a safe bet. But to walk for three days, at 3 mph, that gives a distance of sixty to eighty miles. Did this mean the valley and the bluff was hospitable and filled with prying Egyptians? Today, Moses might request a half-day's walk into the wilderness because the desert is lifeless within ten miles of the valley. No trees. No bushes. No grass. Lifeless.

Yet Moses needed to walk for three days back in his days to find privacy.

Could the Seventh Plague have altered the ecosystem of Egypt? Remember, Israel once was a tropical resort, with forests of cedars, fields of flowers, and capable of hosting flocks that produced vast quantities of milk. Then Nebuchadnezzar laid waste. And then Alexander came. And then Antiochus Epiphanes. Finally, the Romans finished it off by leveling everything in sight. It never bounced back.

[Exodus 9:23] And Moses stretched forth his rod toward heaven: and the LORD sent thunder and hail, and the fire ran along upon the ground; and the LORD rained hail upon the land of Egypt. [24] So there was hail, and fire mingled with the hail, very grievous, such as there was none like it in all the land of Egypt since it became a nation. [25] And the hail smote throughout all the land of Egypt all that was in the field, both man and beast; and the hail smote every herb of the field, and break every tree of the field. [26] Only in the land of Goshen, where the children of Israel were, was there no hail. [27] And Pharaoh sent, and called for Moses and Aaron, and said unto them, I have sinned this time: the LORD is righteous, and I and my people are wicked. [28] Entreat the LORD (for it is enough) that there be no more mighty thunderings and hail; and I will let you go, and ye shall stay no longer.

Then Pharaoh changed his mind, again...

Yet it makes me wonder if this single plague did enough damage to ruin the delicate system, leaving only the valley fertile enough to sustain plants.

Also, notice how this plague is more than just regular hail. This is Emperor Palpatine shooting lightning bolts into the clouds, which then sent fire down to the ground. This is so much more than just a bad storm. Fire does not mingle with hail anywhere except the Book of Revelation (Ch 16). Although the hailstones must not have been massive, they still ripped down every tree. This scene is downright epic to behold.

What's left? Just ego.

The Target:

Egyptian mythology is full of sky gods, so this was not as specific. Besides Ra, we have Nut, the sky goddess and consort of

Geb. Seth is also the god of chaos, so seeing hail and fire together, it was definitely chaotic.

Yet I'd offer Baal. In Ugaritic/Canaanite mythology, Baal is their Thor. He is strong, bold, disobedient, and also chaotic. He is the storm god, whose symbol is the strong bull. Remember that Elijah will also have dealings with Baal worshippers and accepted a challenge to have a God vs. god competition. Although they could have been delusional, it seems to me that they raised their hands and fully expected Baal to accept their sacrifice by having fire come down from the sky to consume it. Don't mess with the true God of physics, I guess. Not only did Baal...bail on them (sorry), but then Elijah taunts them by dousing his offering with water just to show that "natural physics" does not work with the creator of the universe. Baal and the Priests of Baal were taught a harsh lesson that day. So having Moses use his staff to shoot lightning into the sky is pretty much stealing Baal's thunder (sorry for the pun).

Plague Eight: Locusts

Yes more bugs, so I'm looking hard for the symbolism. Apparently, the last plague did not claim all the grass, so the locusts came to finish things off. This plague went over the entirety of Egypt, which is a region more than seven hundred miles north to south. That's a lot of bugs. Besides the devastation, they also get Gingermandias to admit that his enemy (God) is real, powerful, and possibly better than him, but that does not mean he converts or repents.

> **[Exodus 10:12] And the LORD said unto Moses, Stretch out thine hand over the land of Egypt for the locusts, that they may**

come up upon the land of Egypt, and eat every herb of the land, even all that the hail hath left. [13] And Moses stretched forth his rod over the land of Egypt, and the LORD brought an east wind upon the land all that day, and all that night; and when it was morning, the east wind brought the locusts. [14] And the locusts went up over all the land of Egypt, and rested in all the coasts of Egypt: very grievous were they; before them there were no such locusts as they, neither after them shall be such. [15] For they covered the face of the whole earth, so that the land was darkened; and they did eat every herb of the land, and all the fruit of the trees which the hail had left: and there remained not any green thing in the trees, or in the herbs of the field, through all the land of Egypt. [16] Then Pharaoh called for Moses and Aaron in haste; and he said, I have sinned against the LORD your God, and against you. [17] Now therefore forgive, I pray thee, my sin only this once, and entreat the LORD your God, that he may take away from me this death only. [18] And he went out from Pharaoh, and entreated the LORD. [19] And the LORD turned a mighty strong west wind, which took away the locusts, and cast them into the Red sea; there remained not one locust in all the coasts of Egypt. [20] But the LORD hardened Pharaoh's heart, so that he would not let the children of Israel go.

The Target:

I honestly couldn't find much for this one, having used the bug gods for the gnats and flies plague. My only thought is that Apollyon has an army of demons that resemble locusts.

Plague Nine: Darkness

Now it gets extremely paranormal and symbolic. There is nothing natural about these plagues any more. This section is impossible. Fog? No. Thick clouds? No. A meteorite that sends up a cloud of dirt? No.

I'd like to remind Christians (and Jews) that God brought spiritual light on Day One and physical light (from the sun/moon/stars) on Day Four. He brought it with a word. One second, no light; the next second, light. The lighting system was fully formed, just like Adam was fully formed. Clap on...light. Clap off...darkness.

It describes the darkness as something that could be felt, which means that thermal radiation from sources of light defied the laws of physics for three days and the world quickly cooled. Light a fire...no light. Torch...no light. Absolute darkness*.

Except for the Hebrews. While the sun, stars, moon provided nothing for three days, the Hebrews quickly lit fires and these lights were the only source of ambient light in all of Egypt. Or, the Hebrews had "Day One" light in their dwellings, which I believe is the Holy Spirit. Wouldn't that be cool if they just glowed warm with goodness?

Also, there is the point-blank Christ symbolism of three days of darkness. Remember how Christ "harrows" the underworld while dead? Knock, knock? Who's there? Jesus!

[Exodus 10:21] And the LORD said unto Moses, Stretch out thine hand toward heaven, that there may be darkness over the land of Egypt, even darkness which may be felt. [22] And Moses stretched forth his hand toward heaven; and there was a thick darkness in all the land of Egypt three days: [23] They saw not one another, neither rose any from his place for three days: but all the children of Israel had light in their dwellings. [24] And Pharaoh called unto Moses, and said, Go ye, serve the LORD; only let your flocks and your herds be stayed: let your little ones also go with you. [25] And Moses said, Thou must give us also sacrifices and burnt offerings, that we may sacrifice unto the LORD our God. [26] Our cattle also shall go with us; there shall not an hoof be left behind; for thereof must we take to serve the LORD our God; and we know not with what we must serve the LORD, until we come thither. [27] But the LORD hardened Pharaoh's heart, and he would not let them go. [28] And Pharaoh said unto him, Get thee from me, take heed to thyself, see my face no more; for in that day thou seest my face thou shalt die. [29] And Moses said, Thou hast spoken well, I will see thy face again no more.

The Target:

Obviously, if my theory about (Belial=Perdition=Darkness) is true, then this is quite the plague in regards to symbolism. Remember Ra is the sun, Horus is the moon, and Thoth is the, err…god of the moon also. "You have no power here, Gandalf the Gray!"

God is showing Moses, the Hebrews, and us that he has no rival in the universe because…HE CREATED THE UNIVERSE!

Clap on, clap off, the clapper!

Plague Ten: The Destroyer

Imagine that you built a car. You crafted each and every lug nut, bent each panel, and connected all the wires. It is a beautiful machine. Then one day, the tires cry out "I am the master of the car." From the tires' perspective, the car can't do anything without wheels, right?

You scratch your head, looking at your car from the driveway.

Stupid tires.

While it is parked there in the driveway, the wheels and brakes join in this little rebellion, and they all begin to chant "We rule the car! We rule the car!"

Finally, you've had enough. You sit down in the car, insert the key, start the motor, and pull away. Turns out the tires have to do exactly what you want them to do. Their debate meant little. For good measure, you peel out.

I think this is what happens in the 10th plague. In our metaphor, Gingermandias is one of seven lug nuts and Belial is the Tire of Darkness. God built the universe, and He can do whatever He wants with it, right?

So God peels out, leaving little pieces of rubber behind.

[Exodus 11:4] And Moses said, Thus saith the LORD, About midnight will I go out into the midst of Egypt: [5] And all the firstborn in the land of Egypt shall die, from the firstborn of Pharaoh that sitteth upon his throne, even unto the firstborn of the maidservant that is behind the mill; and all the firstborn of beasts. [6] And there shall be a great cry throughout all the land of Egypt, such as there was none like it, nor shall be like it any more. [7] But against any of the children of Israel shall not a dog move his tongue, against man or beast: that ye may know how that the LORD doth put a difference between the Egyptians and Israel. [8] And all these thy servants shall come down unto me, and bow down themselves unto me, saying, Get thee out, and all the people that follow thee: and after that I will go out. And he went out from Pharaoh in a great anger. [9] And the LORD said unto Moses, Pharaoh shall not hearken unto you; that my wonders may be multiplied in the land of Egypt. [10] And Moses and Aaron did all these wonders before

**Pharaoh: and the LORD hardened Pharaoh's heart, so that he
would not let the children of Israel go out of his land...
[Exodus 12:12] For I will pass through the land of Egypt this
night, and will smite all the firstborn in the land of Egypt, both
man and beast; and against all the gods of Egypt I will execute
judgment: I am the LORD. [13] And the blood shall be to you
for a token upon the houses where ye are: and when I see the
blood, I will pass over you, and the plague shall not be upon
you to destroy you, when I smite the land of Egypt...
[Exodus 12:23] For the LORD will pass through to smite the
Egyptians; and when he seeth the blood upon the lintel, and on
the two side posts, the LORD will pass over the door, and will
not suffer the destroyer to come in unto your houses to smite
you...
[29] And it came to pass, that at midnight the LORD smote all
the firstborn in the land of Egypt, from the firstborn of
Pharaoh that sat on his throne unto the firstborn of the captive
that was in the dungeon; and all the firstborn of cattle. [30]
And Pharaoh rose up in the night, he, and all his servants, and
all the Egyptians; and there was a great cry in Egypt; for there
was not a house where there was not one dead.**

The first idea I'd like to discuss is the "firstborn" idea. This is
a lot of death if you include every animal in the land of Egypt.
Remember, a 90-year-old man could be a firstborn, and his 60-
year-old son could be a firstborn, and his 30-year-old grandson
could be a firstborn, and his newborn great-grandson could be a
firstborn. Generations would die in a single night.

It surprised me that the Hebrew word did not specifically
mean firstborn son. Yes, in the patriarchal society, a firstborn
son is important, but the Hebrew word (bekowr), only means
firstborn or chief. Of the 30 translations, only 8 English transla-

tors specified it as male or son. It probably doesn't matter, but Ramses the Great's first child was a daughter, and the passage seems to imply any firstborn of any mammal. If she dies in the 10th plague, then it makes sense why there is a tribute to her built in the land of Goshen. If it was his son, I've got nothing…

Next, ponder the meaning of 12:12. Why is God doing this? It is more than just a Gingermandias thing. He is doing it to execute judgment against the gods of Egypt. That is indeed a jealous God! What gods? All of the above? Dang, this is some heavy stuff happening off camera. There is a cosmic smackdown happening, and the witnesses are all hiding inside.

Lastly, let's talk about the elephant in the room: the destroyer.

The Target:

The Destroyer. Sounds like a Marvel villain, huh? Here, the Hebrew word was **hammashit**, which is a verb rather than a proper noun. In Hebrews 11:28, this scene is summarized with the Greek word **olothreuon**, which is another verb, meaning to destroy, ruin, or perish. So there is not a direct connection to Belial other than the negative connotation of the same meanings.

In Revelation 9:11, we meet an Arch-villain. For some unexplained reason, a bad guy known as Apollyon (in Greek) or Abaddon (in Hebrew) is locked up in the abyss, but is released to lay waste to the world in the End Times.

Just a bit ago, God talked about how he was going to "execute judgment" on the gods of Egypt, yet there is no explanation on what he did. Yet in Rev. 9:11, 9:13-16, and Jude 1:6, there is talk of angels being locked up. If we have giants post flood, there needed to be fallen angels post flood. Yet today, we don't see any, thus...locked up?

God cleaned house on Passover Night, but I'd like to focus on the Angel of Death. If my theory is correct, Belial is the same as Perdition, and Perdition is the same as the Darkness, and the Darkness is the same as Death, and the last enemy is Death.

In the lore of Belial, his name means "he who shall not rise," which means he is deep, like an abyss. In the End Times, he'll be let out to wipe out a world full of his followers. Here, in the era of Moses, God uses IT to wipe out firstborns and possibly deal with the other fallen angels.

How ironic is it that Ramses the Great, Gingermandias, worships the dark gods like Anath, Baal, and Belial, and for the final act, God makes Belial do His dirty work. God does not kill any firstborns, but Belial does.

Remember my car/tire metaphor?

Well, God fires up the engine and shows the tire who is boss. Belial has no choice but to obey the will of God and destroy his own guys.

There is another possibility that I'd like to entertain also, and that is a theory I found in the **Book of Enoch**. In that text, the fallen angels get in trouble for creating the giants, and right as the flood is happening, the archangels show up and kick butt. Ironically, Satan (called Samyaza) did not get in trouble, but another fallen angel, Azazel, took the brunt of the blame. Apparently, it was mostly his plan, and as a result, he was singled out and thrown into a deep pit, which was then covered.

This reminds me of how Apollyon is already locked up and released. Could the scapegoat of Leviticus 16:8 be a connection to the same figure from the **Book of Enoch** (10:8), which later became a symbol of Belial?

Regardless, it was a dark night, and when the sun came up the next day, Gingermandias waved the white flag.

The Hebrews were free!

CHAPTER NINE

TAKING THE ROUNDABOUT

So after four hundred years of dwelling in Egypt (with at least a few hundred in slavery), and a bizarre paranormal battle, the Hebrews are suddenly free...and wealthy.

[Exodus 12:29] And it came to pass, that at midnight the LORD smote all the firstborn in the land of Egypt, from the firstborn of Pharaoh that sat on his throne unto the firstborn of the captive that was in the dungeon; and all the firstborn of cattle. [30] And Pharaoh rose up in the night, he, and all his servants, and all the Egyptians; and there was a great cry in Egypt; for there was not a house where there was not one dead.

And...

[12:35] And the children of Israel did according to the word of Moses; and they borrowed of the Egyptians jewels of silver, and jewels of gold, and raiment: [36] And the LORD gave the people favor in the sight of the Egyptians, so that they lent unto

them such things as they required. And they spoiled the Egyptians.

And...

[12:40] Now the sojourning of the children of Israel, who dwelt in Egypt, was four hundred and thirty years. [41] And it came to pass at the end of the four hundred and thirty years, even the selfsame day it came to pass, that all the hosts of the LORD went out from the land of Egypt.

Did Moses send out a group text? I'm not being facetious, but I really wonder how Hebrew folks found out. From what I can tell, Moses and his family have always lived around the Thebes neighborhood, probably just upstream from the palace. Most of the Hebrews, however, lived down in the land of Goshen. So there is a logistics problem happening here. There are hundreds of square miles of Hebrews to collect.

While it later describes them departing from a town in the Delta, Moses and family would have had to gather up the southern Hebrews and begin heading toward the Delta. The snowball would build as it headed downstream. For Hebrews, it is a celebration, but for the rest of Egypt, it is a terrible day of mourning. God put the bad guys in their place, and all Gentiles, including Gingermandias, submitted to God's authority. In fact, the Gentiles probably slowed the snowball down, for as Moses and crew passed, they had to accept the spoils of victory.

By the time they reached the Delta, the Hebrew population would have been ready to leave. During this time, the Passover tradition was created through necessity. When the snowball rolled by, every Hebrew had to gather up their belongings and quickly bake some bread for the road. While Exodus clearly defines a specific day for the killing of the lamb (Nisan 14th) and the baking of the bread (Nisan 15th), the full Festival of Passover is a seven-day celebration. Why?

The Hebrew Snowball

While seven is a good number, it is impractical to think that all Hebrews baked bread on Nisan 15th because news would not have been delivered via text, right? Consider that the snowball of celebration took seven days to roll from Thebes to the Delta. At each stop, the decree of Gingermandias is heard AND the new religious holiday of Passover is explained. A year later, everybody could do it the same way, but in the first seven days of freedom, the celebration would have been a sloppy mess. Was the EXACT date of the 430 years from Moses leaving Thebes or from the Hebrews leaving the Delta? Not really sure, but somebody like me must've noted it.

> **[12:37] And the children of Israel journeyed from Rameses to Succoth, about six hundred thousand on foot that were men, beside children. 38And a mixed multitude went up also with them; and flocks, and herds, even very much cattle.**

So the biomass of Hebrews gathers up in the Delta, near a place called Rameses. Again, the tone is somber jubilation with a sense of hurry. Moses, for example, had traveled at least four hundred miles in his seven days of travel, which is a reasonable fifty-seven miles a day.

Sound unreasonable? Well, a casual stroll is twenty minutes per mile, meaning you could walk 3 miles an hour. Even with an hour for breakfast, lunch, and supper (to butter your Passover bread?), there would be twelve hours of walking, so a conservative progression would be thirty six miles a day. If in a rush, like the text implies, I think the fifty-seven miles a day is quite reasonable.

With a biomass of two to three million (600K+wife+1 kid=yikes!), pace would certainly be slow. The anachronistic reference to Rameses (Tell el-Daba? Quantir?) and Succoth (Tell-el Maskhuta, El Arish?) also implies that the biomass traveled north. The more conservative location of Succoth means they traveled toward the sea about a distance of thirty-six miles.

What were they expecting?

Roads to the Promised Lands

War, more likely than not. Later, we learn that both Gingermandias and the kingdoms around the Promised Land are surprised when Moses doesn't directly march up the road. After all, there are three ancient roads leaving from the Delta.

The route known as the "Way to Arabia" is the most difficult, cutting across the northern part of the Sinai Peninsula to the upper corner of the Gulf of Aqaba (the right finger in the V-shaped fingers of the northern Red Sea). It is about 200 miles to Aqaba.

The middle route is the "Way of Shur," which goes through some pretty arid regions, passing Masada, the Dead Sea, before directly arriving at Jerusalem. If invasion were the purpose, this would have been the most direct path. It is also about 200 miles to Jerusalem.

The easiest path would have been the route known as the "Way of the Philistines" (Anachronistic, since we don't have Philistines yet). This road is also known as the "King's Highway" because it is a major trade route along the coast, connecting the continent of Africa to Europe and Asia. Even then, they relied on trade. This road would also have been 200-300 miles into the heart of Canaan. Our brick-makers might not have had chariots or horses, but they were plentiful and powerful, capable of overwhelming any opposition with sheer numbers. The "Way of the Philistines" would have given them food and water also.

Instead, God had other plans.

[Exodus 13:7] And it came to pass, when Pharaoh had let the people go, that God led them not through the way of the land of the Philistines, although that was near; for God said, Lest peradventure the people repent when they see war, and they return to Egypt: [18] But God led the people about, through the way of the wilderness of the Red sea: and the children of Israel went up harnessed out of the land of Egypt. [19] And Moses took the bones of Joseph with him: for he had straightly sworn the children of Israel, saying, God will surely visit you; and ye shall carry up my bones away hence with you. [20] And they took their journey from Succoth, and encamped in Etham, in the edge of the wilderness. [21] And the LORD went before them by day in a pillar of a cloud, to lead them the way; and by night in a pillar of fire, to give them light; to go by day and night: [22] He took not away the pillar of the cloud by day, nor the pillar of fire by night, from before the people.

Here is where everything gets messy.

The biomass easily traveled through the Delta from Rameses to Succoth, which was logical and expected. THEN, God shocked everybody. First, he appeared as a pillar, which is pretty obvious, based on the previously "mysterious" ways of God. A father can point at the pillar and shrug, telling his family, "God's leading us." This pillar leads by both day and by night, it seems.

Based on the logical and accepted location of Succoth, there are really only a few directions to go. You can't go north because of the sea. You can't go south because that would lead you up the Nile. You can't go west because that is the way to Libya. You can only go east or southeast. East involves all three highways, which would have made sense.

Instead, God chose "none of the above."

Although the chosen KJV text does not use the words, some newer English translation uses the phrase "the roundabout way" to describe verse 18. The reason is that the Sinai Peninsula is ¾ surrounded by water (Gulf of Suez and Gulf of Aqaba with a bit of Red Sea). Veering to the southeast into the peninsula would mean you'd have to go seven hundred extra miles before you'd end right back in southern Israel.

Even to Moses, who also followed the pillar, this would have been unexpected.

It also would have surprised Ramses.

And the enemies in Canaan.

Only God knew that the Hebrews needed to be spiritually purged before the invasion, and to do this, they needed the 10 Commandments and a good forty years of isolation.

Before Arriving at the Mount...

So far, the only controversial thought I've had is a seven-day explanation for the Passover Festival. Now I'm going to take issue with conventional thought.

What is the conventional thought?

For 1700 years, the accepted route of the Exodus has Moses and the Hebrews traveling into the Sinai Peninsula.

Isn't that what I just suggested? Isn't that the "roundabout" way?

We have a big problem. Before reaching Mount Sinai, Moses and the Hebrews must cross something called "Yam Soph."

The KJV translators read the old Hebrew Yam Soph and translated it as Red Sea. So what's the problem? In the days of the KJV, few Christians had a Bible, let alone a map, or even a Bible map. Modern archeology also did not exist. So when a bunch of evangelized Vikings pictured Succoth and Etham, they just nodded and trusted.

In the last century, we've mostly agreed on the location of Rameses and Succoth, yet if the Hebrews traveled the "roundabout way" and ended up at the accepted location of Mount Sinai, they don't really cross the Red Sea.

What?

The Hebrews were on the eastern edge of the Delta when they departed, right? Then the pillar took them another direction, which either meant southeast, OR...it veered south, then west, then south and back into Egypt, which would have been an act of war! Gingermandias would have freaked out! Only then could they be on the left finger of the V of the Red Sea. Remember, the Suez Canal is a modern creation, so departing from Succoth meant a strange retreat with a biomass of 2 million.

Yet...first cross Yam Soph, then reach Mount Sinai.

Before I deal with my heretical view of Mount Sinai in Chapter 11, I first need to explain my issues with the modern reading of Yam Soph.

A Bitter Theory

To make the modern theory work, the Hebrews need to cross a body of water before ending up at Jabal al Musa (St. Catherine's Monastery a.k.a Mount Sinai a.k.a Mount Horeb). What choices do they have? Again, the zig-zag back into Egypt doesn't work for anybody that I know of, so eliminate that thought.

Instead, the "Bitter Lakes" theory has emerged. For this to work, they need an incredibly slow migration rate, and to also ignore the logical location of Succoth. For, on the edge of the Delta, there is a medium sized lake. Now, in comparison to Minnesota lakes, it is much smaller than Mille Lacs but larger than Lura Lake. Currently (post Suez Canal dredging) it is about ten miles long and seven miles wide. It drains toward the Gulf of Suez, which is the Red Sea, so...kinda the same water?

Scholars have even debated the word (Soph), thinking Red and Reed might be a point of contention. You see, the body of water is known as Great Bitter Lake, and it is a bit of a swamp. It's large but shallow, and as a result, surrounded by reeds. Scholars like it because it is on a path between the Delta and Jabal al Musa, and it is pretty easy for God to separate since it is shallow.

Huh?

Yes, the Bitter Lake theory allows the Creator of the Universe some relief from the heavy lifting. The Red Sea is pretty deep, and Great Bitter Lake is shallow, so God wouldn't have to lift as much water. Or...if you didn't want God to be a visible, active presence (like a pillar of fire), then you could have a "natural" explanation for dividing the water. Say...an earthquake. Or...a tornado! Either of these "natural" phenomena could cause the waters of Great Bitter Lake to part, allowing the Hebrews to escape.

The real miracle is drowning the Egyptian army in such a shallow lake.

You see, the Hebrews would not have been "trapped" in this location. The Egyptians could have seen them on the other side and driven around the Great Bitter Lake. Why risk it? Plus, in Exodus 14:20 describes how it took quite a bit of time (at least all night) for the Hebrews to cross, which does not seem to fit the width of the Great Bitter Lake.

My issues with logic cause other issues. The Great Bitter Lake is still in the Delta, and just a bit off of any logical paths to get to Canaan. Gingermandias would not have seen this as a "change in plan" or even a "foolish plan" from Moses. Plus, on the other side of the Great Bitter Lake, they are still in…Egypt. Prior to crossing Yam Soph, the Hebrews complained that they have been led out of Egypt and into a bad wilderness. Yet, the Great Bitter Lake is still in Egypt. Heck, it is still in the Delta. If you subscribe to the Great Bitter Lake theory, they are twenty miles from the farm fields of the Delta and just fifty miles from the Nile.

The Real Yam Soph

My support for Ramses the Great as the hard-hearted Pharaoh rests in the name of the city of Rameses (which was dedicated to his firstborn daughter), as well as the timing of the 18th Dynasty figures and their motivations. A uniquely "18th Dynasty" trait was the use of bricks for building. Check. Yet if it is indeed the 18th Dynasty, then the capital is Thebes. If

Thebes, then Ramses and all the plagues happen around Thebes instead of the Delta. Check. Even though the text never says Thebes, it does make a distinction that the Land of Goshen was saved from the plagues. In particular, the plague of locusts.

To recap, the locusts were really annoying and ate everything green.

When the plague was over, it describes how a west wind blew the locusts away. Specifically, it blew the locusts into Yam Soph. Again, no locusts in the Delta. Lots of locusts around the Pharaoh. Where was the Pharaoh? Thebes. What is east of Thebes? The Red Sea.

If Yam Soph was meant to be Great Bitter Lake, then the Land of Goshen would have been filled with locusts. Nope. For the locusts to be blown into the Great Bitter Lake, the wind direction would have been almost due north. Nope, the Bible says west. The locusts were blown from Thebes into the large body of water directly east of Thebes, now known as the Red Sea.

Ya see, it doesn't matter whether Soph means Red or Reed. The text defines where Yam Soph should be. It can't be the Great Bitter Lake.

So if Moses and the Hebrews did not cross the Great Bitter Lake, then when and where did they cross any water? It would help to know absolutely where Etham was located, but even without that, look at the text.

[21] And the LORD went before them by day in a pillar of a cloud, to lead them the way; and by night in a pillar of fire, to give them light; to go by day and night: [22] He took not away the pillar of the cloud by day, nor the pillar of fire by night, from before the people.

Again, if you take simple walking pace, and put the Hebrews on the eastern edge of the Delta, and have them go anywhere but one of the three roads, then the above passage would mean they traveled quite a few miles. They could travel by day and night with the pillar of fire, meaning they could easily put on 50 miles a day.

> **[Exodus 14:1] And the LORD spake unto Moses, saying, [2] Speak unto the children of Israel, that they turn and encamp before Pihahiroth, between Migdol and the sea, over against Baalzephon: before it shall ye encamp by the sea. [3] For Pharaoh will say of the children of Israel, They are entangled in the land, the wilderness hath shut them in. [4] And I will harden Pharaoh's heart, that he shall follow after them; and I will be honored upon Pharaoh, and upon all his host; that the Egyptians may know that I am the LORD. And they did so.**

Ignore the place names (since we have no certainty of the locations). God's plan is to do something crazy so that it will appear that they are "entangled," which would bait Pharaoh into changing his mind and reclaiming the Hebrews. Why would he reclaim them? First, they are not attacking the Canaanites, which would have helped him. Second, Moses led them into a location that has "shut them in." Again, this does not match Great Bitter Lake.

What does it match?

Again, if God is indeed leading them to the Red Sea, then they would turn south from Succoth and head directly into the Sinai Peninsula. If you did this, sticking to the Gulf of Suez, you would eventually pin yourself in a sharp peninsula with the Red Sea in front of you.

If God led them by day and night along the Gulf of Suez, then the Hebrews were still technically in Egyptian turf, where dozens of historical mines that provided jewels for the pharaohs were located. The Hebrews would be watched, and mocked, as they marched themselves into a corner. Of course, God had another motive.

Back in Ex 13:7, God said, **Lest peradventure the people repent when they see war, and they return to Egypt.** Again, if you follow the Great Bitter Lake theory, God led them through a swamp to end up in…Egypt. However, if God led them along the Gulf of Suez, toward the tip of the peninsula, then crossing the body of water, the actual Red Sea, would land them in Arabia, which would prevent them from ever returning to Egypt. Isolation mattered to God.

What's in a Name?

The town of Blue Earth is located in Martin County instead of Blue Earth County. The town of Faribault is located in Rice County instead of Faribault County. Mount Sinai is located…?

See the problem?

For the past 1700 years, the dot for Mount Sinai has been Jabal al Musa, located in the middle of the Sinai Peninsula (after all, if you cross the Great Bitter Lake, you've got to find a mountain on the other side). Jabal al Musa is definitely a mountain, but is surrounded by hundreds of other mountains in the middle of a mountainous peninsula. Emperor Constantine's mom, Helena, had put the location of Mount Sinai on maps of Christian sites when she ordered a chapel to be built at the location of the burning bush. By the year 565, it was the location of a monastery, and for the better part of 1,500 years, has been the site of religious pilgrimages.

Why?

Mom said so.

Again, Helena was not Helena Jones, mother of the greatest archeologist known to man, Indiana Jones. She was a tourist. She might have been very devout and saintly, but her credentials? Probably, nothing better than an English degree from Mankato State University.

So what do Helena and I have in common? The Bible.

[Exodus 15:22] So Moses brought Israel from the Red Sea; then they went out into the Wilderness of Shur. And they went three days in the wilderness and found no water.

So...eastern shore of the Red Sea. Check. Wilderness of Shur? Sure. Three days into the wilderness without water. Everywhere along the Red Sea. This line does not help. Let's try another.

[Gen 25:18] And they (Ishmael's descendents) **dwelt from Havilah unto Shur, that is before Egypt, as thou goest toward Assyria: and he died in the presence of all his brethren.**

Havilah is Iraq. Shur? Here, the lands of Ishmael, who is credited as the father of the Arabian people, is described as being East of Egypt. What is on the other side of the Red Sea? Arabia. If Shur was in the Sinai peninsula, it would redefine the Arabian peninsula. But if Shur is the eastern shore of the Red Sea, then this is a perfect description of Arabia.

So Shur=Arabia.

Now go back up and read Exodus 15:22. God led them from the Red Sea into Arabia. Is there anything else to support Arabia? Shur is (sure).

[Galatians 4:22] For it is written, that Abraham had two sons, the one by a bondmaid, the other by a freewoman. [23] But he who was of the bondwoman was born after the flesh; but he of the freewoman was by promise. [24] Which things are an allegory: for these are the two covenants; the one from the mount Sinai, which gendereth to bondage, which is (H)agar. [25] For this (H)agar is mount Sinai in Arabia, and answereth to Jerusalem which now is, and is in bondage with her children. [26] But Jerusalem which is above is free, which is the mother of us all.

So I know Paul is not an archeologist either, but his assumption is that Mount Sinai is...in Arabia. He doesn't explain himself because he is making another point, but notice how he brings up Ishmael via his mom. Ishmael, father of the Arabian people. Arabian people are from...Arabia?

Don't forget, Moses first went to Mount Horeb (Sinai) when he visited the burning bush. Remember why he was hiding? From an Egyptian pharaoh? By leaving Egypt? Well, with the Great Bitter Lake theory, Moses hid in Egyptian territory.

Where is Midian? Midian is up by the Gulf of Aqaba, meaning Jethro/Reuel lives in the NW corner of the Arabian Peninsula. And if Midian is in Arabia, then where is Mount Sinai? Remember, Moses crosses Yam Soph, and then he is suddenly in Midian where he deposits his wife and kids with his father-in-law. It makes perfect sense (except for the miracle) for all of this to be happening in Arabia (sorry, Helena).

CHAPTER TEN

THE BLOOD LICKERS

Time to celebrate! Time to sing!

After a terrible season of plagues, a strange trip on the round-about, and the crossing of the Red Sea, the Hebrews have had quite an emotional ordeal. Standing upon the shores of the sea, a Hebrew horde listens as first Moses and then Miriam sing a song of praise. In this celebration, Moses gives a little regional context to what has happened:

> **[Exodus 15.12] Thou stretchedst out thy right hand, the earth swallowed them. [13] Thou in thy mercy hast led forth the people which thou hast redeemed: thou hast guided them in thy strength unto thy holy habitation. [14]The people shall hear, and be afraid: sorrow shall take hold on the inhabitants of Palestina. [15] Then the dukes of Edom shall be amazed; the mighty men of Moab, trembling shall take hold upon them; all the inhabitants of Canaan shall melt away. [16] Fear and dread shall fall upon them; by the greatness of thine arm they**

**shall be as still as a stone; till thy people pass over, O LORD,
till the people pass over, which thou hast purchased.**

Paraphrase: Wow, Red Sea. Dang, our enemies will freak out. Yay, soon we will go to the Promised Land.

For Moses and most of the Hebrews, they would not be entering into the Promised Land. In fact, it would be another forty years until Joshua and the New Kids on the Block (err...Wilderness) would cross over as Moses assumed.

However, this passage of the song brings up an interesting thought. What were the enemies expecting? Prior to this, Egypt was the uncontested military might in the world. The Theban era of Dynasty 18 took the resources of Egypt, a coalition of nations (Hebrew/Nubian), and the technology of the Hyksos to create an empire second to none.

Yet within this nation, civil war threatened to split it apart. First, it seemed the Deltan vs. Theban royalty would destroy it from within, and then later, the last connection to Nefertiti returns to stoke rebellion again. Even though Moses waged a supernatural battle with Gingermandias, news would have traveled to nearby enemies.

The enemies listed were Edom, Moab, and Canaan. The Edomites were the descendants of Esau, who lived in the extreme southern wilderness of Israel. For them, they would have seen the Hebrew Horde as a threat as it came out of the Sinai Peninsula since they lived south of the Dead Sea and north of Aqaba (the right finger of the Red Sea). While Moses could have taken the two other highways to get to Canaan, the "roundabout" path certainly would have freaked them out, knowing the Hebrews would now pass through their territory. Their concern would work with either the Great Bitter Lake or the actual Red Sea crossing.

The second enemy was Moab. (Cover the kid's ears) Moab is the incest baby of Lot and his daughter. These inbred hillbillies lived along the eastern shore of the Dead Sea. What is strange about the reference to Moab is that they should not have been concerned. If the Hebrews crossed the Great Bitter Lake or even an arm of the Suez, they were not in the path of the Hebrew Horde. If Mount Horeb were indeed where most scholars put it (Jabal al Musa @ St. Catherine's), then the route would never put them into danger or threat. The only way they would be concerned is if the Hebrews were in Arabia, for then, the horde would come out of the desert and into their territory from the south east.

Curious, huh?

Of course, the primary enemy are the Canaanites—for good reason. Whether the Hebrews come from the King's Highway, the peninsula, or from the deserts of Arabia, their goal was clear: regain Canaan. Gingermandias would have loved this. He'd let Moses fight the Canaanites and then come in with his own army to defeat whoever was left.

Instead…Roundabout.

And Egypt lost its most advanced weapon…its chariot army.

The enemies of Egypt would have heard about this disaster for Gingermandias, who would now have to defend his nation from these three enemies while Moses vanished into the wilderness of Arabia. And sure enough…during the forty years of "Hebrew Bible Camp," Gingermandias fights Moab and writes about it on a monument at Luxor. To get to Moab, he'd have to go through Sinai and Edom, yet there is no mention of this during the forty years.

Why?

I believe the Hebrews were somewhere in Arabia away from this mess.

Things move at a pretty quick pace at this time. Within the first three months of the Exodus, quite a few things happen.

Within the first month, they took the Roundabout Way and crossed the Red Sea.

By the 15th day of the second month, they'd received the Sweet Waters, manna, quail, and then some more manna.

By the time they reached the third month, they'd had water from a rock, met Jethro/Reuel, saw Zipporah and her sons return to Midian, and reached THE MOUNTAIN.

That was a lot of stuff to happen.

Sandwiched by those events is one of the strangest encounters of the entire Exodus: the War with Amalek.

Why Attack?

With references to Moab, Edom, and Canaan, it initially reads like the Amalekites are just another nation in their way. However, the archeology of the Sinai Peninsula is strong, and during most of that time, it belonged to Egypt. Thus...the Amalekites were not naturally found in the Sinai Peninsula. If they invaded, then Egypt would be concerned also.

To get to the Hebrews in the Sinai Peninsula, they'd have to come through Moab and Edom, which does not seem to be the case. Also, remember that Moses is in his second home, Midian, where there are...Midianites. So Amalek does not belong any-where near the peninsula or along the coast of the Red Sea.

So why were they even there?

Why pick a fight with the Hebrews when there is no threat *or* practical way to reach them? It is a strange motivation.

We'll talk about the battle in a bit, but for now, remember that there are 600,000 Hebrew men, and Moses needed a su-pernatural boost to win. What gives? Where did so many Amalekites come from?

How did they know where they would be?

Only God knew that the Roundabout plan involved crossing the Red Sea, and the Hebrews were camped in a place without food or water, which meant...no neighbors, right? How did they know where the Hebrews were camped?

Who was Amalek?

Buckle up. Usually, looking up the meaning of Hebrew words prompts yawning, but this word was loaded with amazingly strange possibilities. With any word (see Belial), the variation of emphasis or vowel use can change its meaning, so we'll talk about all the possibilities.

Dweller in the Valley. Again, Moses approaches Midian, where there is a mountain, and thus, a valley. However, his in-laws live in the valley of THE MOUNTAIN, meaning the Ama-lekites had to come from another mountain and another valley, which Arabia seems to lack. Sand, yes. Lots of valleys? Not real-ly.

War-Like. Okay this one is pretty obvious, but in order to have an army, you have to be able to supply it. Moses needed quail, manna, and a watering rock to supply his people, who thought they were going to die, even with God. How did the war-like army of Amalek get supplies?

People of Prey. Cool, huh? Their name means bad guys.

Cave People. Like the Troglodytes? This option confused me a bit, since Jethro has this connection according to Josephus. I would have to flip everything I thought about the Troglodytes and turn them into monsters. But I do think Jethro along with being descendants of Abraham limits this possibility. Hanging out in caves is pretty shady though.

People who lick blood. Seriously. A common rabbinical translation is that Amalek means people who lick blood. Wonder why God gets so specific about blood in the book of Leviticus? What does this imply, though? While the most extreme option crossed my mind (blood, cave, vampire?), it could range from cannibalism to simply preferring their t-bones a little rare. How villainous would the blood lickers be?

Apparently...yup.

Josephus talked about Amalek and used the term **bastards** to describe them, which means we're right back to them being bad guys. However, I'd like to remind the reader of an extreme option. When I read the Book of Enoch, the giants of Genesis 6 were called either biters or bastards, depending on the translation. Could Amalek have a connection to giants? Well, the Arabian word Imlik is singular for giant, and considering where I think this story is talking place, and where it is heading (see Chapter 5), I think there is something VERY ODD about this encounter.

The Battle

So after crossing the Red Sea, running out of food and water, and not yet to THE MOUNTAIN, Amalek comes out of the blue to challenge the Hebrews. Here is how it goes:

[Exodus 17:8] Then came Amalek, and fought with Israel in Rephidim. [9] And Moses said unto Joshua, Choose us out men, and go out, fight with Amalek: to morrow I will stand on the top of the hill with the rod of God in mine hand. [10] So Joshua did as Moses had said to him, and fought with Amalek: and Moses, Aaron, and Hur went up to the top of the hill. [11] And it came to pass, when Moses held up his hand, that Israel prevailed: and when he let down his hand, Amalek prevailed. [12] But Moses' hands were heavy; and they took a stone, and put it under him, and he sat thereon; and Aaron and Hur stayed up his hands, the one on the one side, and the other on the other side; and his hands were steady until the going down of the sun. [13] And Joshua discomfited Amalek and his people with the edge of the sword. [14] And the LORD said unto Moses, Write this for a memorial in a book, and rehearse it in the ears of Joshua: for I will utterly put out the remembrance of Amalek from under heaven. [15] And Moses built an altar, and called the name of it Jehovahnissi: [16] For he said, Because the LORD hath sworn that the LORD will have war with Amalek from generation to generation.

Paraphrase: Moses used a paranormal technique involving a golden staff to defeat Amalek and his people.

And...onto THE MOUNTAIN.

Hold on a bit. What is going on in this battle? An army of 600,000 Hebrews is losing to Amalek? In fact, it takes another miracle for the Hebrews to win. Now, I looked up Rephidim, which does not have any archeological support for a specific location (I'll let it go), but while I was looking up the word, I stumstumbled across the Hebrew word for attacked...way ·yil ·lā ·ḥem. What does this word mean? To feed on, to consume, to battle. YIKES!!!! The blood lickers were feeding on them? Holy Cow! (intentional Baal pun).

I keep coming back to the worst definition possible, don't I?

Hyperbole. It MUST be an exaggeration. Luckily, God helps Moses win, and the Hebrews defeat Amalek. How many Hebrews died? Not sure. How many men did Amalek lose? Not sure. Did Joshua put Amalek to the sword? Also not clear. One thing that is clear is that Amalek will be back.

Cuz God said so.

Look closely at what God said, and it might leave you chilled. After making an altar to the victory, Moses explains what God said. **I will utterly put out the remembrance of Amalek from under heaven** and later **the LORD will have war with Amalek from generation to generation.** How do you put out remembrance? Under heaven? God must not like this Amalek, for he continues to say he will make war with Amalek from generation to generation. Considering archeologists still don't know who these guys were at the time, nor did we see them become a great enemy like Babylon or Rome later, Amalek does not do his part with the war. Yet this is a promise from God...Amalek will be back!

From Generation to Generation

Strangely, the account in Exodus 17 seems to indicate a person...Amalek. This is fine in just the context of this battle, but given the context of God waging war with him from generation to generation, I need a bit of context.

Genesis 14:7 makes a reference to the land of the Amalekites. Yes, this is the section where the coalition of kings are fighting giants before turning on each other in a civil war that claims Lot as a prisoner. Chronologically, this would have been several hundred years earlier. Does that mean Amalek was alive then? Or...since Moses wrote Genesis, is that just an anachronistic reference like Rameses?

A few generations later, Esau's grandson is named Amalek, which is why many scholars claim they are the same. The math would make our Amalek over 500 years old, which is quite strange. Is he an immortal? According to Nachmanides, Esau is actually named AFTER a previous Amalek, which is like a Viking naming his son Thor. Folks knew of Amalek from lore.

In Numbers 14:45, the Amalekites and Canaanites joined forces to attack the Hebrews who defied their "time out." This happened right after the spies returned with tales of Giants, and upon refusing to trust God's plan, the rebellious Hebrews were told it would be 40 years before God would deliver Canaan to them (actually, just their kids). So some bold Hebrews decided to invade without God's help, only to be killed by the Amalekites (who were in Canaan now?)

By Numbers 24:20, it seems the "time out" is almost over, and the exile is nearing the end of the forty years. Here, the prophet Balaam brings up that **"Amalek was the first of all nations, and shall be last until he perishes."**

What?!?

How can Amalek possibly be considered the first nation? Heck, Nimrod should be the first nation post flood. Does this mean Amalek predates Nimrod? And how is Amalek going to be the last nation? Look at the world today? Any mention of Amalek? What is going on with this chapter?

Amalek does not go away, and Saul must face him in 1 Samuel 15. When he spares King Agag, Saul loses favor with God. This is the reason why God turns to David. How badly does God want Amalek wiped out? He's serious! But why?

Theories on Amalek

The theories vary widely. I read one theory that claims that Haman from the Book of Esther was an Amalekite, and thus, the war continued from generation to generation. Another theory believed that Sennacherib assimilated the Amalekites into the Babylonian/Persian bloodlines. During the Armenian genocide, the Amalek prophecy was used as an excuse to "kill 'em all." Jewish tradition explains that organized atheism is the proper way to interpret our war with Amalek. I even came across a theory, based on some loose language, that connected Amalek to Lamech (from Genesis). I guess this would make the city-builder the first nation, and his bloodline (carrying Cain's DNA) is why we still have bad guys.

So I offer the Willis theory, knowing there is not much consensus on crazy.

Take a look at:

[Revelation 9:13] And the sixth angel sounded, and I heard a voice from the four horns of the golden altar which is before God, [14] Saying to the sixth angel which had the trumpet,

Loose the four angels which are bound in the great river Euphrates. [15] And the four angels were loosed, which were prepared for an hour, and a day, and a month, and a year, for to slay the third part of men. [16] And the number of the army of the horsemen were two hundred thousand thousand: and I heard the number of them. [17] And thus I saw the horses in the vision, and them that sat on them, having breastplates of fire, and of jacinth, and brimstone: and the heads of the horses were as the heads of lions; and out of their mouths issued fire and smoke and brimstone. [18] By these three was the third part of men killed, by the fire, and by the smoke, and by the brimstone, which issued out of their mouths. [19] For their power is in their mouth, and in their tails: for their tails were like unto serpents, and had heads, and with them they do hurt.

Who are the four angels buried under the Euphrates?

Why are the four angels buried under the Euphrates?

(Drax voice) What are the four angels buried under the Euphrates?

Consider that for giants to exist, you need a fallen angel. The offspring of a fallen angel and human host are bastards and/or biters. What if Amalek once was an angel? During the Great Flood (according to the ***Book of Enoch***), the bad guys were thrown into the Abyss. Yet Satan and others were not locked up. Evil continued to exist. The Hyksos people, after a brutal defeat to the Egyptian coalition, retreat to the Promised Land and regroup. Their plan? Enlist help, and the answer to their dark prayers is Amalek.

Amalek and his monster babies come out of the desert to ambush Moses, who needs to use supernatural efforts to defeat a supernatural force looking to devour them. When over, God promises that the war is not over. Why? Because when the pillar of fire precedes the Ark of the Covenant on Year 1 of the Joshua regime, the four fallen angels (including Amalek) are locked up in a prison under the Euphrates. Just as Balaam predicted, Amalek will not perish until the War of Armageddon. His release happens in Revelation 9.

From Joshua to King Saul, God tries to purge the foul abominations from humanity in a war that sounds like genocide yet is far darker. The Canaanites somehow survive, and the War with Amalek goes on for generation to generation.

It's an epic theory, at least.

CHAPTER ELEVEN

LIVING IN SIN

So our omniscient God led the Hebrews by the "roundabout" way, through Yam Soph, and directly into the path of a pretty horrible enemy, the Amalekites, all while knowing that the Hebrew spies would lose their nerve after seeing what waited for them in the land of Canaan.

The plan?

Bible camp.

Remember that the Hebrews have been immersed in Deltan, Hyksos, and Theban culture for the better part of four centuries, and as a result, they have probably developed some pretty skewed beliefs. By contrast, Jethro and Zipporah remained people of God despite being Midianites, who were not the "chosen people." Down in Nubia (a.k.a. Cush, Aksum, Sheba, Ethiopia), there remained more "God folks" who still had texts like *Adam and Eve* and *The Book of Enoch*, who would present themselves in Israel in the form of the Queen of Sheba and would celebrate their connection to David/Solomon for centuries afterwards. The Hebrews, however, needed to go to a spiritual rehab center.

Even though after three months they had seen LOTS of supernatural signs and wonders, the Hebrews still did not have a clear "moral code." Most folks are very familiar with the Ten Commandments (which is why I'm leaving that for Sunday School), but the Hebrews were also about to receive the **Book of Leviticus**, which goes into minute detail to explain what offends God. Even though Christ later explained that these rules condemned **everybody**, a definition was needed.

This is a sin…

This is also a sin…

Stop doing this…it's a sin too.

Although Moses was righteous (he already had his spiritual rehab from age 40 to 80), the Hebrews would also need their forty years. Remember, they did not WANDER for forty years; they WAITED for forty years so their kids could enter into the Promised Lands. The older generation had seen too much sin, and the younger generation needed to be brought up in isolation from other cultures. Spiritual rehab.

In Exodus 18, Moses seems to understand this, and during a meeting with Jethro, explains how he is burdened with answering questions and making judgments. Because of this burden, Moses leaves his wife and sons with Jethro and pushes deeper into the wilderness.

> **[Exodus 19:1] In the third month, when the children of Israel were gone forth out of the land of Egypt, the same day came they into the wilderness of Sinai. [2] For they were departed from Rephidim, and were come to the desert of Sinai, and had**

pitched in the wilderness; and there Israel camped before the mount.

By this time, you're probably sick of me complaining about the "reality" of the migration, but here is another example of how the rate of even a simple walking pace would make it problematic for any size of horde to stay within such a small area as the "Sinai" peninsula. After crossing the Red Sea, it seems that there are several more days of journey, adding an additional month to year one of the Exodus. The peninsula is only about 200 miles long, which is a bit problematic for more than a week of travel. If you go with my theory about actually crossing Yam Soph, then the Hebrews really find themselves stuck deep in the Arabian Peninsula.

Without God, they'd be dead in days.

Until recent centuries, when transportation and technology "shrunk" the world for travelers, the old maps created of the Middle East showed the location of Mount Sinai as Jabal al Musa, also known as St. Catherine's monastery. Again, I have nothing against this being the Holy Mountain except for the minimization of the listed miracles, the dramatically slow travel rate, and the illogical interactions of faces and places described in the text. It just perplexes me, and the traditional location just seems...off.

Here are a few things bouncing around in my little mind.

Would God want the "Holy Mountain" to be public or hidden in mystery?

What were the characteristics described in the Bible about "The Mountain"?

Who else ever went to "The Mountain"?

So this chapter is going to focus more on the meaning of "Sinai" and the "Wilderness of Sin" rather than the commandments.

The Name of the Mountain

After a thousand years of acceptance, there are now some crackpots (am I included?) challenging the placement of the Holy Mountain of God. My reasons are to be as adherent to the text as possible, not to criticize, but just to understand. So let's start by looking at what the name means.

In some places, it is called HOREB. Horeb is a reference to glowing, heat, or the sun. So this makes perfect sense. When Moses stands in front of the angel, the bush appeared to burn but didn't burn from a natural flame. Horeb. The "Horebing" Bush.

This is a nice title.

More often than not, it is also called Mount Sinai. Remember, the only reason we call it the Sinai Peninsula is because Constantine's Mom (Helena) put a pin in the map at Jabal al Musa.

Was there archeological proof?

I could open Google Earth, get out my distance line, and take a stab at it also, but that won't mean I am right. The problem with most of this section of Exodus is that there is no conclusive acceptance since God dropped them into a place where there were no other humans. Plus, the Hebrews never built any permanent houses. For a creative fellow like me, there are all sorts of possibilities.

So what does "Sinai" mean?

Sinai comes from the phrase "Wilderness of Sinai" or "Wilderness of Sin" and "Wilderness of Zin." This word is also used in association with Kadesh, which is also disputed. Many scholars have put their pins in the map to justify the Helena theory, much to my chagrin.

First, let's look at the Hebrew word used for Wilderness, mid bar. This word implies "desert" yet the peninsula is very mountainous, especially around Jabal al Musa. For this reason, scholars have often placed it in extreme southern Israel, allowing the rest of the peninsula to be dubbed Sinai.

By comparison, Arabia is a more classic definition of desert. Remember my earlier references to Arabia? Is there a connection? It turns out there is a Sumerian deity named Sin (aka Nanna). Where is Sumer? It was ancient Babylon, in the land of Ur, where Abram came from. So if Moses wanted to explain where the Hebrews stayed, and he was in Arabia (which I think there is support), then writing "Wilderness of Sin" would translate into "the sandy area between me and Iraq," which would be…the Arabian Desert.

Yes, my theory would need to redefine Rephidim and Kadesh, but I think it makes a lot of sense for why the Hebrews will later have to cross the Jordan River. Putting them in the Arabian Desert also provides isolation and complete dependence on God. When they leave, the sands cover up all traces of their stay.

But THE MOUNTAIN should still be somewhere, right? The mountain did not evaporate when the Hebrews left.

The Holy Mountain of God

This very special mountain that Moses visited might be special for some other reasons. In Ezekiel, there is a very strange passage that seems to compare the King of Tyre directly to Satan. While ignoring the elephant in the room (Satan), notice the little tidbit included in

> **[Ezekiel 28:13]: Thou hast been in Eden the garden of God; every precious stone was thy covering, the sardius, topaz, and the diamond, the beryl, the onyx, and the jasper, the sapphire, the emerald, and the carbuncle, and gold: the workmanship of thy tabrets and of thy pipes was prepared in thee in the day that thou wast created. Thou art the anointed cherub that covereth; and I have set thee so: thou wast upon the holy mountain of God; thou hast walked up and down in the midst of the stones of fire.**

The holy mountain of God? If all of this angel talk is indeed Satan in the Garden of Eden, then it connects Satan with something not mentioned in Genesis, a mountain. Sure enough, in the **Book of Enoch** as well as **The Book of Adam and Eve** (which is a strange Ethiopian version of Genesis), there are expanded descriptions of the Holy Mountain of God. To paraphrase, after Adam and Eve left the Garden of Eden, they went to a mountain with a cave, where they found shelter in their early days. Remember the magi? Well, there is a backstory about the treasures of gold, incense, and myrrh, which were housewarming gifts as well as prophetic messages of hope. The message? Keep these gifts and regift them to the Christ when he comes. Then the story explains how it turned into a tomb for Adam and other preflood patriarchs. The mountain also had a "window of heaven" above it, where Adam and Eve could look up to see into Heaven.

Junk, huh? Well, ask yourself why Moses included this detail about the flood in Genesis 7:20 "**Fifteen cubits upward did the waters prevail; and the mountains were covered.**" Why do we need to know how deep the floodwaters were? Did Moses measure? What is significant about fifteen cubits? Deep enough to drown a giant? Well, what if the Holy Mountain of God from Ezekiel matched the other two accounts? If true, then the window of heaven was fifteen cubits above the Holy Mountain of God. The floodwaters unnaturally came from the "fountains of the deep" and the "window of heaven" instead of regular rain clouds. If the "window of heaven" is like a faucet, then Moses understood how deep the floodwaters were…fifteen cubits. So now Moses and Ezekiel seem to connect their mountain talk (weak evidence, though).

If the Holy Mountain of God existed BEFORE the flood, would it have been destroyed? If it did survive the scouring flood, would it still be special? Or found? Later, I'll talk about the "precautions" Moses took with the mountain, but know that if any unrighteous person set foot on it while Moses was talking with God, they would fall down dead. Epic, huh?

Elijah Visits Mount Horeb

There are some really cool details found in 1 Kings involving Elijah , that wild prophet who later takes a chariot ride into Heaven and vanishes from the earth (see John the Baptist for more details). In this section, Elijah is tormenting the unrighteous Ahab and Jezebel, who want him killed. Like Moses, he goes into hiding. Like Moses, he goes to Mount Horeb.

[1 Kings 19:1] And Ahab told Jezebel all that Elijah had done, and withal how he had slain all the prophets with the sword. [2] Then Jezebel sent a messenger unto Elijah, saying, So let the gods do to me, and more also, if I make not thy life as the life of one of them by tomorrow about this time. [3] And when he saw that, he arose, and went for his life, and came to Beersheba, which belongeth to Judah, and left his servant there. [4] But he himself went a day's journey into the wilderness, and came and sat down under a juniper tree: and he requested for himself that he might die; and said, It is enough; now, O LORD, take away my life; for I am not better than my fathers. [5]And as he lay and slept under a juniper tree, behold, then an angel touched him, and said unto him, Arise and eat. [6] And he looked, and, behold, there was a cake baken on the coals, and a cruse of water at his head. And he did eat and drink, and laid him down again. [7] And the angel of the LORD came again the second time, and touched him, and said, Arise and eat; because the journey is too great for thee. [8] And he arose, and did eat and drink, and went in the strength of that meat forty days and forty nights unto Horeb the mount of God.

[9] And he came thither unto a cave, and lodged there; and, behold, the word of the LORD came to him, and he said unto him, What doest thou here, Elijah? [10] And he said, I have been very jealous for the LORD God of hosts: for the children of Israel have forsaken thy covenant, thrown down thine altars, and slain thy prophets with the sword; and I, even I only, am left; and they seek my life, to take it away.

[11] And he said, Go forth, and stand upon the mount before the LORD. And, behold, the LORD passed by, and a great and strong wind rent the mountains, and brake in pieces the rocks

before the LORD; but the LORD was not in the wind: and after the wind an earthquake; but the LORD was not in the earthquake: [12] And after the earthquake a fire; but the LORD was not in the fire: and after the fire a still small voice. [13] And it was so, when Elijah heard it, that he wrapped his face in his mantle, and went out, and stood in the entering in of the cave. And, behold, there came a voice unto him, and said, What doest thou here, Elijah? [14] And he said, I have been very jealous for the LORD God of hosts: because the children of Israel have forsaken thy covenant, thrown down thine altars, and slain thy prophets with the sword; and I, even I only, am left; and they seek my life, to take it away.

[15] And the LORD said unto him, Go, return on thy way to the wilderness of Damascus: and when thou comest, anoint Hazael to be king over Syria: [16] And Jehu the son of Nimshi shalt thou anoint to be king over Israel: and Elisha the son of Shaphat of Abelmeholah shalt thou anoint to be prophet in thy room. [17] And it shall come to pass, that him that escapeth the sword of Hazael shall Jehu slay: and him that escapeth from the sword of Jehu shall Elisha slay. [18] Yet I have left me seven thousand in Israel, all the knees which have not bowed unto Baal, and every mouth which hath not kissed him.

Okay, so there is a lot to take in from that section (FYI, Malachi 4:4 confirms Elijah at Horeb). First, I'd like to point out that Elijah went one day into the wilderness from Beersheba (which is indeed in the southern part of Israel/Judea). Which direction was that? It does not say if he went south (toward Jabal al Musa) or east (into Arabia). Beersheba is on the edge of the Negev desert, and just twenty miles from the present day border of Egypt. Elijah is 180 miles from Jabal al Musa.

To prepare him for the rest of his journey, an angel arrives and bakes him a cake. As strange as this sounds, I think there is something significant happening. Whether he is about to travel to Jabal al Musa or into Arabia, it will be a tough trip. Like the Hebrews, he is getting "angel food cake," which will sustain him the exact same way manna sustained them. It is a heavenly food that allows him to go day and night into a place where there is no food or water. Super cool.

Now, this is where math again causes some issues for me. Elijah is supernaturally charged up with angel food, allowing him to travel both day and night. He did not have to go slowly or lazily with a horde of Hebrews with him. In contrast, Elijah, by himself, could walk at a brisk pace (4-5 mph). The text implies that he did not lounge around on long breaks. So I'm going to give him eight hours to sleep (and since he does not have to stop for breakfast, lunch, or dinner), he could easily be walking 16 hours a day.

For how long?

Holy cow! (Baal joke). If I even dial that down to 10 hours a day, he would travel fifty miles a day for 40 days, which would be 2,000 miles! Oh, dear! He just flew past Jabal al Musa, didn't he? The pace for Jabal al Musa would be 4.5 miles PER DAY!!!!!! How big is the Arabian peninsula? 1,400 miles from Beersheba to the side closest to the Indian Ocean. Again, one theory limits reason and the other seems to fit.

There are a few other things to note in the Elijah story.

First, there is a cave. Now, the Moses story does not mention a cave, but here, Elijah distinctly adds this detail, which seems to match the strange preflood accounts. A second detail found in the account is the idea of holy fire, but that is not natural...only when God arrives. The earthquake is curious since it could change the landscape of the mountain.

Yet the coolest detail (for my theory) is that God tells him to swing by Damascus on his return. Returning from Egypt (Sinai Peninsula) would take him through Judea and Israel, but returning from the deserts of Arabia, he would come out of the wilderness at Damascus. Pretty cool.

Jesus at Horeb?

The forty-day journey along with "angel food" reminded me of the account of Jesus being tempted in the wilderness. What wilderness? Well, defenders of Jabal al Musa put the "Wilderness of Sin" near Egypt, which is pretty close, if I'm being honest. Matt 4, Mark 1, and Luke 4 all describe Jesus going into the "wilderness," but only the gospel of John says where Jesus had been prior to leaving: the wedding at Cana. If the spirit led Jesus into the wilderness, he would have gone all the way back south from Galilee and into Judea, etc. Some scholars just have him hang in Galilee in the mountains. I'd like to propose that Jesus went to Mount Horeb (not in Sinai but Arabia).

Elijah took forty days to get to Mount Horeb, and here, Jesus "fasted" and was "led" for forty days and forty nights. What it doesn't say is if Jesus walked for two miles, and sat down for the next 39 days OR...if he walked for 39 days and sat down on the fortieth. None of the accounts are clear about that. I do know that angels had to "minster" (nourish) him afterwards, so the journey was difficult. Passing from Galilee to the south would have allowed him to pass through civilization for much of the journey. Walking into the wilderness of Arabia would have left him quite vulnerable (which seemed the point of the temptation). The next anecdote after the temptation has Jesus returning to Jerusalem at the Passover before returning to Galilee to get his flock. Forty days there and back again would give you about 80 days, and with the days specifically described by John around the wedding of Cana and baptism, it would mean Jesus was baptized just after the Feast of Dedication in Jerusalem. Having Jesus take the same trip as Elijah is not only super symbolic (post John the Baptist's baptism) but it also gives a tight account of the three months between winter and spring. If you have Jesus go anywhere else, the days don't add up to fill the three months.

Moses at the Mountain

So there are several passages that describe the mountain. Let's do a quick overview to refresh our memories. When Moses is given the 10 Commandments, there are some interesting details:

[Exodus 19:11] The people will be able to see God descend on Horeb.

[Exodus 19:12] Moses put "bounds" around the mountain to keep them safe.

[Exodus 19:18] Smoke and fire surrounded the top

[Exodus 33]: After the golden calf, they buried their loot at the mountain.

Much of Exodus 19-end concerns laws and regulations, but by the end of it (Chapter 40), the first year of the Exodus comes to an end, with God appearing as a pillar of smoke/fire, signalling if they'd move the camp or not.

But where is the mountain?

The Helena Theory has them staying in a triangle of land 100 miles wide by 100 miles wide. The Arabia theory gives them the vast wilderness of Arabia to hunker down.

Problems with the Helena Theory

In 330 A.D., after a site-seeing tour of the Holy Lands, St. Helena built a chapel at Jabal al Musa, which would later become known as St. Catherine's Monastery. FYI, Catherine of Alexandria was beheaded and angels hid her body (like Moses in Chapter 12). In 800 AD, monks found her body and built the monastery, which became a popular stop during the crusades.

Problem #1: There is not a lot of space. While the pillar could have them moving a few miles east and a few miles north and a few miles south, the peninsula is a pyramid shape. Too far west, and you're right next to Egyptian mines. Too far east and you're in Midian or Moab. The mountain ranges also mean "the camp" would be spread out over a vast area of ravines and valleys.

Problem #2: It is still Egypt. The whole point of rehab is to break them of their pagan addictions. The Helena theory puts them less than 100 miles from Goshen. They could run away and be back in Egypt in just a few days.

Problem #3: Ramses is only 56 when Moses is 120. That's right, Ramses the Great did not die in the Red Sea. He could have grown an entirely new army and gone back for the Hebrews. The Great Bitter Lake? That ain't stopping him. In the Sinai Peninsula, the Hebrews are still stuck between a rock and a hard place. Gingermandias could make war on them for four decades. Moses hurt his pride. Why would he stop hating the Hebrews?

Problem #4: Have you looked at Google Earth? The terrain around Jabal al Musa is 1,200 square miles of rugged mountains. There is nothing different about Jabal al Musa than a thousand other peaks near it. The ravines are steep. There is nowhere to put 600,000 Hebrew men, regardless of how many died during that first year. Jabal al Musa itself has no "viewing area" where the Hebrews could see God descend. Heck, based on seating, most of the Hebrews would have been behind several mountains. There is no good place to encircle the mountain with rocks either. It does not stand alone.

Problem #5: It has tourists. Moses had to put rocks around the mountain to keep Hebrews from dropping dead by standing too close. Now, there is an airport, steps, railings, trashcans, and a panoramic viewing area.

The Jabal al Lawz Theory

So after years of thinking the map in my Bible did not match what it seems to describe, I came across a book by Howard Blum called **The Gold of Exodus.** In the NYT best seller, he writes about the travels of Larry Williams and Bob Cornuke as they disregarded the Helena Theory in favor of an actual crossing of the Red Sea into Arabia.

So far, so good.

In the book, they felt the "roundabout" way was dipping into the peninsula to cross the Red Sea at Sharm al-Sheikh (the tip) and into Arabia.

Works for me.

Then the adventure tale matched up details from Exodus that seemed too good to be true. They claimed to find chariot wheels in the channel, and then matched Exodus detail for detail (Marah, Elim, etc). Finally, they arrived at a place known as Jabal al Lawz, which according to locals, was the real place where Moses received the LAW. There are rocks that seem to have unique water erosion. There are Solomon's markers commemorating the crossing. The mountain stands alone and even has a sooty, dark top.

It really, really matches.

In the book, Williams and Cornuke are trying to evade the Saudis, who have a top-secret military base built near the mountain. Why? Because the nation of Israel also knows the Helena Theory is wrong and the Lawz Theory is right, and out of holy respect, will not bomb the area. While sneaking around, they claim to have found all the right stuff: the border stones, the cave, and even the pits where the Hebrews left their Egyptian booty. Because of antiquity laws passed right about the setting of the adventure, Saudi Arabia could not "claim" the discovery for fear of the gold going back to the country of origin (a court battle between Israel and Egypt). So rather than letting either enemy win, they kept it hushed.

It was a great read.

Others have jumped on the bandwagon in the past few decades, including the same guy, Ron Wyatt, who claimed to find Noah's Ark (not the one in Kentucky) on Mount Ararat. While I fully believe the Arabia Theory makes sense, I am not entirely convinced of the Lawz Theory. Something just feels shady about the new theory.

The Arabia Theory

None of the above?

While little makes sense about the Helena Theory or Great Bitter Lake theory, there are a few passages that make me question Jabal al Lawz also. There is so much room in Arabia that there could be any mountain. Remember Elijah? Jabal al Lawz is still too close for him to walk into the wilderness 40 days. Jabal al Musa is 182 miles and Jabal al Lawz is...182 miles also. Yet Jabal al Lawz and Arabia makes a lot more sense for these reasons:

1. Ramses the Great could no longer reach them.
2. Egypt would need to use its regular army to invade Edom, Moab, and Midian to even come close to finding the Hebrews.
3. No Hebrew could choose to walk away without risking being captured by the above enemies.
4. Arabia is a land without detail (Rephidim, Kadesh, Sin, Zin, etc).
5. There is no food or water in the Arabian desert (manna).
6. The Hebrews cross the Jordan from the east. Arabia is east. Helena's mountain is south.
7. **Exodus 3**: Mount Horeb is described as being near Midian, along the "back" of the desert. Moses was hiding from Pharaoh Horemheb. If Midian is near Aqaba, then it would be strange that Moses would flock closer to Egypt (Jabal al Musa). It would make more sense if he flocked from Midian deeper into Arabia.
8. **Exodus 19**: Once the Hebrews pass by Midian, they reached the mountain. The Helena theory would have

them looping around in the Sinai Peninsula. The Arabia theory would have them just going deeper into Arabia.

Psalm 106:19 and Deuteronomy 5:2 also use the word Horeb without any tangible clues, but Deuteronomy 1 gives me some very cool details. In this chapter, Moses is 120 years old and the forty years of rehab are finally over. Since year 1, the Hebrews have been hunkered down eating manna and drinking from a rock. Where? Somewhere without archeology or landmarks.

> **[Deut 1:1] These be the words which Moses spake unto all Israel <u>on this side</u> Jordan in the wilderness, in the plain over against the Red sea, between Paran, and Tophel, and Laban, and Hazeroth, and Dizahab. [2] (<u>There are eleven days</u>' journey from Horeb by the way of <u>mount Seir</u> unto <u>Kadeshbarnea</u>.) [3] And it came to pass in the fortieth year, in the eleventh month, on the first day of the month, that Moses spake unto the children of Israel, according unto all that the LORD had given him in commandment unto them; [4] After he had slain Sihon the king of the Amorites, which dwelt in Heshbon, and Og the king of Bashan, which dwelt at Astaroth in Edrei: 5On this side Jordan, in the land of Moab, began Moses to declare this law, saying, [6] The LORD our God spake unto us in Horeb, saying, Ye have dwelt long enough in this mount: [7] Turn you, and take your journey, and go to the mount of the Amorites, and unto all the places nigh thereunto, in the plain, in the hills, and in the vale, and in the south, and by the sea side, to the land of the Canaanites, and unto Lebanon, unto the great river, the river Euphrates. [8] Behold, I have set the land before you: go in and possess the land which the LORD sware unto your fathers, Abraham, Isaac, and Jacob, to give unto them and to their seed after them.**

Kadesh Barnea? Not really sure (lack of archeology) but it is in a wilderness somewhere.

The Jordan River? That one's easy. It runs distinctly north to south and acts as a border (along with a mountain range) between Israel and the rest of the Arabian peninsula. Mount Seir? That is in the land of Moab. With the Helena Theory, the Hebrews stayed near Jabal al Musa for forty years, and then traveled straight north. At no point is this on the "other side" of the Jordan River since it is due south. To get on the wrong side of the Jordan, Moses needed to veer too far east, only to have Joshua cross back over again. An eleven day journey meant a pace of a dozen miles PER DAY.

With the Arabia theory, they are always on the "other side" of the Jordan River (i.e. east of it vs. south). For them, at a reasonable pace, an eleven-day journey to arrive in Moab could be 300 miles, placing Horeb deep in Arabia. This 11 day journey is another reason why I struggle with Jabal al Lawz (too close to Mount Seir/Moab).

Numbers 20 brings the Exodus to a close. After forty years of rehab, the Hebrews were ready to go into the Promised Land. The Helena theory would mean they would travel straight north and then cross into Moab and Edom so they could cross the Jordan River (between Galilee and Dead Sea). The Arabia theory would mean they came out of the Arabian desert to arrive right at the N/S natural border, the Jordan River.

[Numbers 20:14] And Moses sent messengers from Kadesh unto the king of Edom, Thus saith thy brother Israel, Thou knowest all the travail that hath befallen us: [15] How our fathers went down into Egypt, and we have dwelt in Egypt a long time; and the Egyptians vexed us, and our fathers: [16]

And when we cried unto the LORD, he heard our voice, and sent an angel, and hath brought us forth out of Egypt: and, behold, we are in Kadesh, a city in the uttermost of thy border: [17] Let us pass, I pray thee, through thy country: we will not pass through the fields, or through the vineyards, neither will we drink of the water of the wells: we will go by the king's highway, we will not turn to the right hand nor to the left, until we have passed thy borders.

[18] And Edom said unto him, Thou shalt not pass by me, lest I come out against thee with the sword. [19] And the children of Israel said unto him, We will go by the highway: and if I and my cattle drink of thy water, then I will pay for it: I will only, without doing anything else, go through on my feet. [20] And he said, Thou shalt not go through. And Edom came out against him with much people, and with a strong hand. [21] Thus Edom refused to give Israel passage through his border: wherefore Israel turned away from him.

Helena Theory: Edom would not block them. In fact, they could easily access the King's Highway from Jabal al Musa just by heading north. Edom is south of the Dead Sea. Yet with this theory, the Hebrews still manage to sneak through Edom to somehow end up on the eastern side of the Dead Sea and River Jordan. Huh? "No, you can't pass through our territory" yet then in Chapter 21, they magically appear in Moab. So they did cross through Edom? Or...

Arabia Theory: To come out of Arabia, and reach Canaan, you'd have to pass through Edom to reach the King's Highway. From the southeast, Edom lies between the Dead Sea and the Gulf of Aqaba. Edom blocks the way for a generation of Hebrews who have never experienced violence. These folks are young and holy.

Avoiding war with Edom, Moses and the Hebrews bounce north, to the land of Moab, which borders the Dead Sea. This makes sense if they came from Arabia. This is impossible if they came from Jabal al Musa.

To the evil Canaanites, who'd been waiting for the invasion for 40 years, the weakest link in defending their land was from the south, where there is no geographic advantage. An alliance with Edom kept the Hebrews from doing the obvious. Heck, Ramses the Great would have made an alliance with Canaan to crush the Hebrews along the King's Highway. Instead, Moses and the Hebrews bounce to the north, eventually reaching the Jordan River, which was one of the steepest rivers on earth. This was a natural border, and even if they managed to cross, the mountains would have given them high grounds pleasing to Obiwan Kenobi (Episode 3 pun).

Yet once again, God leads the Hebrews to the worst possible spot...and then performs a miracle. The only thing left to do, though, is to wait for Moses to die.

CHAPTER TWELVE

MORTE D'MOSES

From the Hyksos invasion to the rehab in the desert, the Exodus era witnessed some of the strangest times in history. For 120 years, Moses was the figure at the center of it. The plan seemed to involve more than just freeing a people from bondage; instead, a cosmic battle occurred to put evil back in its place. Starting with the gods of Egypt, Moses went toe-to-toe with the priests of Belial. Before the plan could finish, the Hebrews needed to have faith, resulting in forty years of isolation to learn how to be righteous. Now, with Gandalf, err...Moses, leading the fellowship across the Jordan River, the Hebrews were about to finish the fight.

The accounts of the Exodus mostly focus on year one and year forty. Much of that has to do with the fact that Moses was in the tabernacle and the Hebrews just hung out, eating manna and learning the Bible, which was coming hot off the press daily. Somewhere in the wilderness, the Hebrews would move camp from time to time but mostly stayed in complete isolation. When they finally popped up from the toaster, they were eleven days from Edom. Here are some highlights of the key events:

[Numbers 20]: Moses denied the Promised Land

[Deut 3:27]: A duplicate account of Moses whacking that rock with too much style.

[Num 33]: Israel prepares to cross the Jordan.

[Deut 24:33]: Israel warned to remember Amalek

[Deut 31]: Joshua chosen to lead Phase B

[Deut 34]: Moses dies on Mount Nebo

Since the death of Moses is the focus of our chapter, and this book focused mostly on Moses, let's examine it a bit.

[1] And Moses went up from the plains of Moab unto the mountain of Nebo, to the top of Pisgah, that is over against Jericho. And the LORD shewed him all the land of Gilead, unto Dan, [2] And all Naphtali, and the land of Ephraim, and Manasseh, and all the land of Judah, unto the utmost sea, [3] And the south, and the plain of the valley of Jericho, the city of palm trees, unto Zoar. [4] And the LORD said unto him, This is the land which I sware unto Abraham, unto Isaac, and unto Jacob, saying, I will give it unto thy seed: I have caused thee to see it with thine eyes, but thou shalt not go over thither. [5] So Moses the servant of the LORD died there in the land of Moab, according to the word of the LORD. [6] And he buried him in a valley in the land of Moab, over against Bethpeor: but no man knoweth of his sepulchre unto this day. [7] And Moses was an hundred and twenty years old when he died: his eye was not dim, nor his natural force abated. [8] And the children of Israel wept for Moses in the plains of Moab thirty days: so the days of weeping and mourning for Moses were ended.

[9] And Joshua the son of Nun was full of the spirit of wisdom; for Moses had laid his hands upon him: and the children of

Israel hearkened unto him, and did as the LORD commanded Moses. [10] And there arose not a prophet since in Israel like unto Moses, whom the LORD knew face to face, [11] In all the signs and the wonders, which the LORD sent him to do in the land of Egypt to Pharaoh, and to all his servants, and to all his land, [12] And in all that mighty hand, and in all the great terror which Moses shewed in the sight of all Israel.

While disappointing that Moses could not finish things (metaphor), these verses certainly remind us of how awesome Moses was.

City of Palms: First, I want to point out that Moab's geography is MUCH different than today. Again, go to Google Earth, and you'll see an arid wasteland, yet 3,000 years ago, Moses looked down upon a paradise of sorts. My point: if Moab/Jordan was this much different, then perhaps the southern parts of Israel were better, and if the southern parts of Israel were better (like Beersheba/Negev), then the definition of "wilderness" should be applied to Arabia.

His sepulchre: For the most famous Hebrew prior to Christ, it is a very strange thing not to commemorate his tomb. Keeping it a mystery has obvious logic. We'll get back to this one.

120 Years Old: Was it the whacking the rock or his age that disqualified him? I say this because WAY back in Genesis 6, there is a much disputed phrase that either means God will bring the flood in 120 years OR...the natural lives of humans are now capped at 120 years. Many folks like the warning because the 120 cap was "grandfathered" into humanity. A tapering of ages began immediately, but even Abraham lived to 175. Was

Moses the first one to not reach 121? Did the system begin then?

His natural force: Paul writes about being reborn and regaining our original flesh, which will be perfect. Although Moses was born with "fallen" flesh, he nonetheless stood in the purifying fires of God and also ate manna for forty years. Despite being 120, he was still in good shape. He was not withered and weak. He was still strong. This is why I ponder the 120 year rule.

Face to Face: Oh, boy, do I have things to say about this one. First, let's get back to the burial.

A Strange Death

When it says no man knew where Moses was buried, it implies that an angel showed up to take care of the duties. Enemies would have plundered it; fans would have worshipped it. Origen, a famed historian, wrote about the account being found in **The Assumption of Moses**. While referenced in the days of the early church, an actual copy was not found until recent years, with many scholars rolling their eyes at it. While it is a bit odd, St. Jude might have had an original copy that he referenced in:

> **[Jude 9] Yet Michael the archangel, when contending with the devil he disputed about the body of Moses, durst not bring against him a railing accusation, but said, The Lord rebuke thee.**

Jude's argument was how to handle evil folks, but in making his point, he brings up a very strange account of how Michael and Satan got in an argument about the body of Moses. Whether it was just guarding the tomb or a Law and Order trial of "worth," we'll never really know, but it is certainly a curious and slightly epic finish to our hero.

The Jesus Tent

Again, the end of Deuteronomy gives Moses a nice send off, but when it said "the LORD knew face to face," my brain-springs popped out of my ears. What?

Exodus 3:2 is the first time Moses has a God-moment, but it varies from saying "Angel of the Lord" to a direct "LORD" en-counter. Much later, Exodus 33:11 references that the LORD spoke to Moses face to face, as a man speaks to his friend. Very cool, but WHAT?!? Exodus 34:34 adds more of the same when it brought up a "veil" to dial down the holiness when speaking with the Hebrews but that he would "take it off" to speak with God. Face to face with God?

Luke dials this down a bit with his account in:

[Acts 7:37]: This is that Moses, which said unto the children of Israel, A prophet shall the Lord your God raise up unto you of your brethren, like unto me; him shall ye hear. [38] This is he, that was in the church in the wilderness with the angel which spake to him in the mount Sina, and with our fathers: who received the lively oracles to give unto us:

The angel which spake to him?

The reason I freak out about the wording here is the absolute clarity of two other verses. First, look at

[Exodus 33:20] And he said, Thou canst not see my face: for there shall no man see me, and live. [21]And the LORD said, Behold, there is a place by me, and thou shalt stand upon a rock: [22] And it shall come to pass, while my glory passeth by,

that I will put thee in a clift of the rock, and will cover thee with my hand while I pass by: [23] And I will take away mine hand, and thou shalt see my back parts: but my face shall not be seen.

Here, God clearly wants to avoid killing Moses and "dials" things down for him.

Next, let's look at John Thunderson (sounds Norwegian...John, the son of Zebedee. You know, the disciple). After an epic Jesus is God, the Word, Creator opening to Chapter 1, John goes on to say in verse:

[John 1:17] For the law was given by Moses, but grace and truth came by Jesus Christ. [18] No man hath seen God at any time; the only begotten Son, which is in the bosom of the Father, he hath declared him.

So right after clarifying that Jesus=God, John clarifies that Moses did not see God. So who did Moses see?

The Metatron

No, not the *Transformers* villain. The metatron is an old Jewish concept that might explain seeing God without seeing God. According to tradition, this messenger is some sort of heavenly scribe. Some see him as Enoch "transformed" while others clarify he is an angel but not God. The title means "Name like his Master" which is why the burning bush scene involves both an angel and the LORD.

Theophanies

Christian scholars noted the same concept throughout the Old Testament. In some places, it was just an angel, yet other places, it was the Angel of the Lord. There were several places where God revealed himself to man, such as incidents with Adam & Eve, Cain, Noah, Moses, a bunch of prophets, a bad guy (Balaam), and of course, David.

The Angel of the Lord appears 103 times (I did not personally confirm this). Early church fathers quickly theorized (read John 1) that this phrase might have meant the pre-incarnate Christ. Prior to being born in Bethlehem, Christ existed and witnessed the creation and Fall of Satan. Theordoret (another scholar) assumed that the Angel was probably Christ without human form. Eastern fathers clarified that the "Word of God" should be seen as Jesus the Christ (prior to taking flesh). Protestant theologians called this the Christophany, while Jehovah's Witnesses saw these appearances as both Jesus and Michael.

It is an abstract concept, isn't it?

Having the Christ visit Moses allows this strange contradiction to exist. John is right when he says no man has ever seen God's face, and Moses is right when he claims to have seen a face (which belongs to the Christ). Remember, Jesus and Moses actually meet in the Gospels.

[Matthew 17:1] And after six days Jesus taketh with him Peter, and James, and John his brother, and bringeth them up into a high mountain apart: [2] and he was transfigured before them; and his face did shine as the sun, and his garments became white as the light. [3] And behold, there appeared unto them

Moses and Elijah talking with him. [4] And Peter answered, and said unto Jesus, Lord, it is good for us to be here: if thou wilt, I will make here three tabernacles; one for thee, and one for Moses, and one for Elijah…

…but I say into you, that Elijah is come already, and they knew him not, but did unto him whatsoever they would. Even so shall the Son of man also suffer of them.[13] Then understood the disciples that he spake unto them of John the Baptist.

First, I want you to remember that both Elijah and Moses had been to Mount Horeb, which is why I think Jesus went out into the same wilderness to be tempted by the devil at the same mountain. Is this the same mountain above? Mostly likely not, since the six days do not allow enough natural travel. But who knows with Jesus?

In this scene, Jesus meets with two heavyweights of the Old Testament, shows his true form to the disciples, and seems to "gear up" in advance of the crucifixion. Now, remember that Moses was clearly dead, which seems to imply that Elijah is also dead, with the only explanation (in this book) was that Elijah died when John the Baptist died (buy ***Examining Christmas*** for more). The supernatural lights on a mountain remind me so much of the supernatural lights on a mountain top (Horeb). Did John, Peter, and James witness the same "face of God" that Moses claimed to see…Jesus. Remember, this is Jesus "transfigured" and thus he would glow.

So when you picture Moses in the tabernacle for forty years, and the pillar would appear above the tent, picture the transfigured Christ sitting face to face with Moses. After all, Jesus is the WORD. What did Moses do in the tent, he wrote WORDS. In the beginning…

Jesus at Horeb

This is not the only time Jesus and Moses came together in the Gospels. When he goes into the wilderness (which I believe to be Horeb) to be tempted for forty days, Jesus does something most are not aware of...he battles Satan with Moses.

Yes, the WORD was in the tent, Moses wrote the WORDS down, and thirteen centuries later, Jesus repeats the same WORDS that he originally gave to Moses. Weird, huh?

[Luke 4:1] And Jesus being full of the Holy Ghost returned from Jordan, and was led by the Spirit into the wilderness, [2] Being forty days tempted of the devil. And in those days he did eat nothing: and when they were ended, he afterward hungered. [3] And the devil said unto him, If thou be the Son of God, command this stone that it be made bread. [4] And Jesus answered him, saying, It is written, That man shall not live by bread alone, but by every word of God. [5] And the devil, taking him up into an high mountain, shewed unto him all the kingdoms of the world in a moment of time. [6] And the devil said unto him, All this power will I give thee, and the glory of them: for that is delivered unto me; and to whomsoever I will I give it. [7] If thou therefore wilt worship me, all shall be thine. [8] And Jesus answered and said unto him, Get thee behind me, Satan: for it is written, Thou shalt worship the Lord thy God, and him only shalt thou serve. [9] And he brought him to Jerusalem, and set him on a pinnacle of the temple, and said unto him, If thou be the Son of God, cast thyself down from hence: [10] For it is written, He shall give his angels charge over thee, to keep thee:[11] And in their hands they shall bear thee up, lest at any time thou dash thy foot against a stone.[12] And Jesus answering said unto him, It is said, Thou shalt not

tempt the Lord thy God. [13] And when the devil had ended all the temptation, he departed from him for a season.

So, long story short, Jesus won, using the words of Moses as a shield. Remember how Jude warned us about debating Satan, and how Michael only said "the Lord rebuke you" as his passive-aggressive defense? Well, Jesus goes toe-to-toe with Satan in a classic courtroom battle worthy of Perry Mason (for you boomers out there). Let's look at what I'm talking about:

[Deut 8:3]=Bread Alone

[Deut 6:16]=Worship only God

[Deut 6:13]=Do Not Tempt

This confirms that the "textus receptus" scriptures given to Moses were validated by Jesus when he used them against Satan.

Cool.

Somewhere, Mary and Joseph and a very proud Sunday School teacher were smiling. Okay, so Jesus had the Holy Spirit descend upon him already, but as the non-transfigured Christ, I'm not sure how much of his human brain he relied upon or if he had Holy Spirit-Sirri to help. It is a test. It is temptation. Jesus passed the test.

However, there is a very, very strange use of the words of Moses here. Satan quotes Moses. Now, Satan may or may not be "in the loop" with what's going on. After all, he was actively part of a dialogue between himself and God in testing Job, right? How much did he know about the "Christ Plan"?

Like Job, Satan tried to catch this Jesus fellow in some sort of legalese "gotcha" moment. Did Satan just think Jesus was a dude from Nazareth and very much like Job? Did he have a clue that the Window of Heaven opened up above John the Baptist,

God spoke, and the Holy Spirit descended upon Jesus. This is like an episode of Undercover Boss! Satan is being bad, thinking it is a substitute teacher, only to find out that God is watching behind those Hebrew eyes. Heavy stuff!

Yet when testing Jesus, Satan brings up a line about the Christ. He brings up the "rules" that the real Christ will be able to command the angels. It is my belief that Revelation 12 is a flashback that parallels Luke 10:18. So in this scenario, Satan has already had his butt kicked by the Christ and the angels, and was thrown down to earth. Here, he wants non-glowing Jesus to flex his Christ muscles a bit, which Jesus refused and passed the test.

HOLD YOUR HORSES!

Psalm 91 is about the Christ?

Leave it to Satan to not only lose, but to screw up while losing.

For many Christians, they view Psalm 91 in a very personal way. The Bible is awesome like that, isn't it? It was written for a specific context but often has layers of meaning. Best writing in human history. As an English teacher, what else has poetry, symbolism, plot twists, and bracketing that takes place from multiple POV characters yet weaves together into one cohesive story.

Yet King David did not write all the "songs" in Psalms.

In fact, you can see that Psalm 90 has a heading/break that introduces a new writer, Moses (remember Moses broke into song after the Red Sea). Because of this, and the heavy use of Moses in the temptation, the author of Psalm 91 is most likely Moses. Normally, I use the old King James Version in my studies just to contrast the English from four centuries ago to today's versions. However, when I had my "lightbulb" moment, I had a New King James Bible, so I'm going with that in this case. It is my theory that Moses wrote this Psalm to express the mind-blowing concept that THE WORD came to the tent to give him THE WORDS that would become the Bible so that THE WORD could use THE WORDS when he comes to earth in the flesh to save Moses from death/the underworld. Moses celebrates this time-bending concept in a song. Since Moses is the writer, his voice is represented by the "I/first person." Since he is referencing Christ, the "you/second person" is Jesus. This leaves God as "he/third person." Below each verse, I will give you my modern paraphrase.

[91:1] He who dwells in the secret place of the Most High
Shall abide under the shadow of the Almighty.

Translation: The Christ currently hides in God's secret place (See Rev 12:5)

[2] I will say of the Lord, "He is my refuge and my fortress;
My God, in Him I will trust."

Translation: Moses trusts God's plan

[3] Surely He shall deliver you from the snare of the fowler
And from the perilous pestilence.

Translation: God will protect the Christ from Satan during a trial

[4] He shall cover you with His feathers,
And under His wings you shall take refuge;
His truth shall be your shield and [b]buckler.

Translation: God will cover Jesus with the Holy Spirit. Jesus will use the Bible as defense against Satan.

[5] You shall not be afraid of the terror by night,
Nor of the arrow that flies by day,
[6] Nor of the pestilence that walks in darkness,
Nor of the destruction that lays waste at noonday.

Translation: The Devil will do everything he can to stop this plan, but if Jesus trusts God, the plan will work.

[7]A thousand may fall at your side,
And ten thousand at your right hand;
But it shall not come near you.

Translation: Slaughter of the innocents in Bethlehem? Joseph left first.

[8] Only with your eyes shall you look,
And see the reward of the wicked.

Jesus shall be surrounded by sin yet will not sin...thus ending the Job debate.

[9] Because you have made the Lord, who is my refuge,
Even the Most High, your dwelling place,
[10] No evil shall befall you,
Nor shall any plague come near your dwelling;

Translation: Jesus went to a holy place. Could be the temple, his local synagogue, or even MOUNT HOREB. Because Jesus trained in righteousness, he will get to fulfill the entire plan, which means getting to the cross.

[11] For He shall give His angels charge over you,
To keep you in all your ways.
[12] In their hands they shall bear you up,

Lest you dash your foot against a stone.

Translation: The angels are loyal to the Christ. If called upon, they will answer. Up to the temptation, there is no evidence that this has happened. Once the temptation ends, the angels show up. Later, Jesus commands the seas, demons, etc.

[13] You shall tread upon the lion and the cobra,
The young lion and the serpent you shall trample underfoot.

Translation: Not certain. Lion and cobra seem symbolic. Young lion is symbolic. If I were to take a stab at it, I'd say this is code for Belial, Beelzebub, and Satan. Jesus will crush the head of Satan, and the last two enemies are Death and Hades. 3 symbols=3 enemies.

[14] "Because he has set his love upon Me, therefore I will deliver him;
I will set him on high, because he has known My name.

Translation: Because Christ has visited me, Moses, and gave me the words for Deuteronomy, I will help him out during the temptation. I will help Jesus win because Jesus visited me here in my tent. Jesus will quote me!

[15] He shall call upon Me, and I will answer him;
I will be with him in trouble;
I will deliver him and honor him.

Translation: Jesus will call for me, Moses, and even though I will be dead at the time, I will visit him on some anonymous mountain for the transfiguration. Because of this little pep talk, Jesus will have the strength to finish the plan, which is crucifixion.

**[16] With long life I will satisfy him,
And show him My salvation.''**

Translation: I, Moses, will live for a long time (120 years) yet will live again during the transfiguration, and then be restored when Jesus harrows him from Sheol.

That is the way to end a book on Moses. Moses dies, but ultimately, helps defeat the bad guy. When Jesus dies, He does not die in defeat. Instead, he victoriously goes down into Sheol to get Moses and other righteous dead.

Amen!

Well, I hope you enjoyed reading this. I know I'm always looking for the most EPIC way to see things, and in my ZEAL for the Lord, I might have misread or misunderstood passages. I don't need to be right, but writing this has allowed me to immerse myself in the WORD. It's a good place to be.

ABOUT THE AUTHOR

Jason Lee Willis, a self-described Luth-olic-a-tist, characterizes himself as "just a nerd with a Bible" and has led adult and youth small group studies at home and at church for the past three decades. As a former English teacher who explored literature to find possibilities rather than absolute answers, Willis looks for "out of the box" interpretations with a preference for the most "epic" answers. While versed in world mythology and history, he remains the son of the church secretary raised in a conservative small town.

The Miracle Alchemist

TRANSFORM YOUR LIFE WITH 4 KEY STEPS TO CREATE MIRACLE-LICIOUS MANIFESTATIONS

BERNADETTE RODEBAUGH